Fireworks 8

Right from the Start

R. Chasemore

PAYNE-GALLWAY
From Harcourt

Published by Payne-Gallway Publishers Limited
Payne-Gallway is an imprint of Harcourt Education Ltd
Halley Court, Jordan Hill, Oxford, OX2 8EJ

Copyright © Richard Chasemore 2007
First published 2007

11 10 09 08 07
10 9 8 7 6 5 4 3 2 1

British Library Cataloguing in Publication Data is available from the British Library on request

10-digit ISBN: 1 905292 22 8
13-digit ISBN: 978 1 905292 22 6

Ordering Information
You can order from:

Payne-Gallway, FREEPOST (OF1771),
PO Box 381, Oxford OX2 8BR
Tel: 01865 888070
Fax: 01865 314029
E-mail: orders@payne-gallway.co.uk
Web: www.payne-gallway.co.uk

Contents

About this Book

You will learn how to create original artwork for a wide variety of purposes using **Fireworks**, one of the components of the **Macromedia Studio** suite.

The screenshots and instructions refer to **Fireworks 8** and **Microsoft Windows XP**. **Fireworks 8** is very similar to **Fireworks MX**, and those using the latter should have little difficulty doing the exercises in this book.

What is Fireworks?

Fireworks is a graphics design package that incorporates many features that are ideally suited to web page creation. Mastering graphics software is a challenge. With step-by-step instructions and hot tips from a professional graphic artist, you will soon be expert in using Fireworks!

Getting Fireworks

If you don't already have Fireworks installed, you can purchase a copy or download a fully working 30-day trial version from **www.adobe.com/uk/products/fireworks/**.

Additional Software

Fireworks is produced by Adobe within its Macromedia range of web development application software, such as Flash and Dreamweaver. This book does not assume that you have any of these other programs.

The Scenario

Throughout this book you will work on sample exercises to create and develop graphics for a company called **Base Camp**, which is an activity club for children aged between 9 and 14. You will be asked to produce a range of graphic products for the club.

The exercises use some photographs to work on as examples. You can download these from the Payne-Gallway website (you'll be talked through this later).

Figure 1.1 ©Acorn Adventure

Using the exercises, you will learn how to design and produce the following.

- ◗ **A logo for Base Camp**, which will include a scan of your preliminary sketches, annotated to show how you developed your ideas. The logo will use at least three colours, will be scalable without losing detail and will work in colour or monochrome.

- ◗ **A birthday card**, which will be given to children who have birthdays while at the camp. It should be identifiable as a **Base Camp** birthday card. For this piece of work, you will also make a hand-drawn mock-up of the real card. You will show the dimensions and scale of the card and show how you used a grid to ensure the picture was correctly positioned on the front of the card.

- ◗ **A Base Camp dollar note**, which will be used instead of money inside the camp. You will learn how the image should be prepared for printing (specifying the resolution, size and colour system) so that it will look how you want it to.

- ◗ **A web page**, which will be based on the graphics you have designed in earlier examples.

Software

You will be using Macromedia Fireworks 8 throughout this book, but as it is very similar to Fireworks MX you will have no difficulty following the instructions whichever version you use. Fireworks 8 is a component of Studio 8, an updated version of Studio MX.

File-naming conventions

It is a good idea to decide on a convention for naming folders and files – and to stick to it. All the folders and files used in the exercises will use a convention called 'CamelCaps', where each word in the file or folder name will start with an uppercase letter, but they will not use spaces or underscores in file names.

Creating a folder structure

You need to create a folder structure to hold all the various graphics, documents, scans and source material that you accumulate while doing the exercises. This can be created using Microsoft Windows Explorer. Here is the structure that you should use.

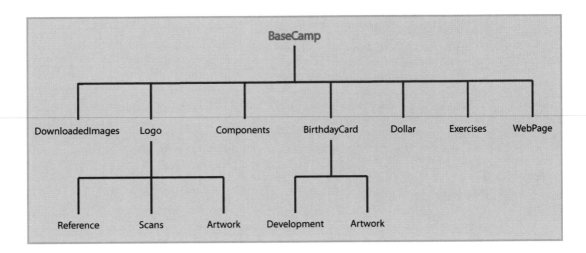

Figure 1.2: The folder structure

DownloadedImages

This folder will contain images that you download from various sources for use in your project. These might include, for example, photographs that you manipulate or use in a montage.

Logo

This folder will contain three subfolders: **Reference**, **Scans** and **Artwork**. **Reference** will be used to save other logos or graphics that you use as reference material to help you form your own ideas. **Scans** will be used to save scans of your hand-drawn sketches. **Artwork** will be used to save versions of the logo and any other artwork you develop as part of the corporate image.

Components

This folder will contain images that may be used in more than one piece of final artwork – for example, a montage that is used on a web page and on a birthday card.

BirthdayCard

This folder will contain two subfolders: **Development** and **Artwork**. You will create and photograph a mock-up of your birthday card and the photos can be saved into **Development**. You will also use this folder to save a screenshot of the grid you use. **Artwork** will be used to save the various versions of your birthday card.

Dollar

This folder will contain the artwork for your Base Camp Dollar.

Exercises

This folder will be used to save any other files that you create as you work through the book.

WebPage

You will use this folder to save files you create as you develop the Base Camp website.

Creating the folder structure

Create a folder structure in Microsoft Windows Explorer that matches Figure 1.2.

▶ Open **Windows Explorer** by right-clicking on the **Start** button and clicking **Explore** on the pop-up menu that appears.

Figure 1.3: Opening Windows Explorer from the Start menu

▶ Find a suitable place to put your folders. This will probably be somewhere in **My Documents**.

▶ Create a new folder in the usual Windows fashion and call it **BaseCamp**.

▶ Create the subfolders beneath the **BaseCamp** folders to match Figure 1.2.

Your folder structure should now look like this:

Figure 1.4: The exercise folder structure

Elements table

It is a good idea to keep a record of all the images you use or create. This helps you to keep track when you are working with large projects, such as websites. An example is shown in Figure 1.5.

Image (file name)	Primary/ Secondary Source	Bitmap/ Vector/ Combination	Description	Source details	Produced by	Where used	Permission (how obtained if required)

Figure 1.5: Example of an Elements table

Introduction to Fireworks

2

Getting started

Fireworks is a versatile graphics art package. You can use it to create, edit and optimise both bitmapped and vector images. It is primarily aimed at web page designers, so you can quickly and easily create hyperlink buttons, rollover images and pop-up menus as well as creating and editing graphics using a range of effects.

Let's get started!

▶ Load Macromedia Fireworks 8. You can do this one of two ways.

1. Either double-click the **Fireworks** icon on the Desktop.

2. Or click **Start** at the bottom left of the screen, then click **All Programs**. When the programs pop up, click **Macromedia** and then select

Macromedia Fireworks 8

Your screen will look like this:

Figure 2.1: The opening screen

Menu bar: This contains menus organised by topic. The **Help** option on this menu is useful for getting extra information on a particular topic.

Tools panel: This is docked down the left side of the screen. It is where you will choose the tools to create or edit your pictures.

Properties inspector: This will initially show document information and will display options and properties when you select an **object** or **tool**.

Panel dock: This area contains a range of powerful **panels**. Panels can be opened and closed from the **Window** menu.

Document window: This is the workspace. It can be thought of as the artist's canvas.

Start page: This pops up when you start a new session with Fireworks and displays recently opened items as well as shortcuts to download tutorials from the Adobe website. You can click the **Don't show again** box to stop it from popping up.

The Tools panel

The **Tools** panel is organised into six sections or categories: **Select**, **Bitmap**, **Vector**, **Web**, **Colors** and **View**.

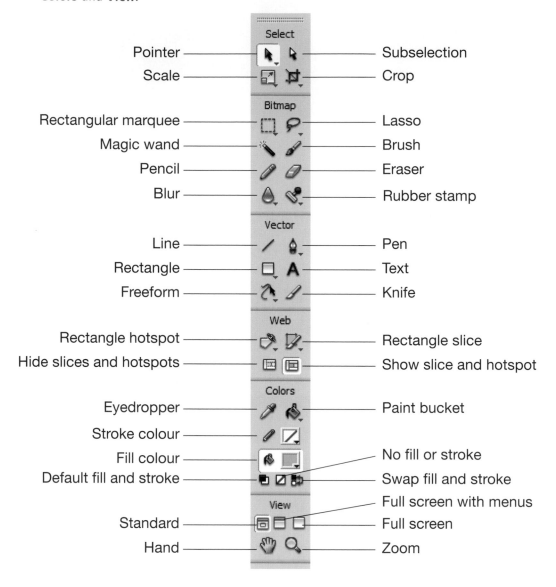

Pointer	Subselection
Scale	Crop
Rectangular marquee	Lasso
Magic wand	Brush
Pencil	Eraser
Blur	Rubber stamp
Line	Pen
Rectangle	Text
Freeform	Knife
Rectangle hotspot	Rectangle slice
Hide slices and hotspots	Show slice and hotspot
Eyedropper	Paint bucket
Stroke colour	No fill or stroke
Fill colour	
Default fill and stroke	Swap fill and stroke
	Full screen with menus
Standard	Full screen
Hand	Zoom

Figure 2.2: The Tools panel

Until a new document is opened, the **Tools** panel icons appear dimmed. They will only become active when a file is opened.

Some of the tools have further options (indicated by a small triangle in the bottom right corner of the tool button). These options can be viewed by holding down the mouse button as you click and selecting from the choice displayed.

Creating a new document

You can create a new file from the **Start page** by selecting **Create New, Fireworks File**.

Alternatively, go to the **Menu** bar and choose **File, New**.

○ Create a new file now. The **New Document** dialogue box will appear, showing default settings.

Figure 2.3: New Document dialogue box

○ Set the **Width** to **1000 Pixels**, the **Height** to **750 Pixels** and the **Resolution** to **72 Pixels/Inch**.

Tip: 72dpi (dots per inch) is usual for most computer screens, but if you are creating graphics for printing then you may need to use a higher resolution (common settings are 300dpi and 600dpi).

○ Set the **Canvas color** to **White**. This is the most suitable colour for the image you are going to create.

Tip: Make sure you have selected **Pixels** and **Pixels/Inch** in the drop-down lists. Fireworks may initially have assumed **Centimeters** and **Pixels/cm**.

○ Click **OK**.

Your screen will look like this:

Figure 2.4: Blank canvas

The Brush tool

The **Brush** tool is a painting tool. The width of the brush, the amount and density of the paint on the brush and how it behaves all depend on the settings in the **Properties inspector**.

◉   Select the **Brush** tool from the **Tools** panel.

◉   Click and drag the paintbrush on the canvas to see the effect.

> **Tip**: If you press **Shift** while drawing with the **Brush** tool, the brush will be locked on a horizontal/vertical/45-degree plane. If you hold down the **Shift** key and click around the canvas, the **Brush** tool will draw a series of straight lines.

The **Properties inspector** is used to pick colours and options.

> **Tip**: If the **Properties inspector** panel is not visible, go to the **Menu** bar and select **Window**, **Properties**. The panel will look slightly different according to the tool you choose.

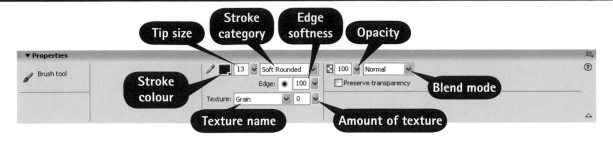

Figure 2.5: Properties inspector

◑　On the bottom right of the **Properties inspector** there is a white triangle. Click it to switch between the full-size option and the half-size option.

◑　Now collapse the **Properties inspector** by clicking the **black triangle** on the left of the **Properties inspector** title bar. Click it again to expand it. These options will be useful later when you have a more crowded workspace.

◑　Click on the coloured square in the **Properties inspector** (the **Stroke color** box) and click on a colour from the pop-up window – something like a dark blue is best for the next stage.

Figure 2.6: Colour pop-up window

◑　Change the **Tip size** in the box next to the **Stroke color** box and note that the brush changes size.

Tip: When you click the **Tip size** box you will see a slider, which you can move up or down to increase or decrease the size of the brush. You can check the size of the brush by moving the mouse pointer over the canvas: an outline of the brush will show you its size and position. You can type a number in the **Tip size** box instead of using the slider if you find that quicker.

○   Change the **Edge** to harden or soften the **Brush** tool edges.

○   Now change the **Opacity** (see Figure 2.5) to alter the amount of paint flowing through the brush.

○   Click the **Stroke category** box and choose **Charcoal**, **Textured**. Try painting!

Figure 2.7: Choosing a Stroke category

○   You can change the texture in the brush stroke by clicking the **Texture** box and choosing another texture. Use the slider next to it to increase or decrease the effect.

The **Blend mode** is something we will look at later, but you can try selecting different options and painting on the canvas – the effect will be more noticeable if you paint over lines you have already drawn.

The Zoom tool

○   Click the **Zoom** tool (the bottom right icon in the **Tools** panel). You will notice the mouse pointer has turned into a magnifying glass with a plus sign in the middle.

○   Click on your canvas to zoom in on your drawing so you can add some detail. Keep clicking as far as it will go.

Figure 2.8: Pixels

The squares that make up a picture are called pixels. When you created this canvas, you specified that it should be 1000 pixels wide and 750 pixels high.

○ Press and hold the **Alt** key and notice that your magnifying glass now shows a minus sign. Click the canvas and you will zoom out.

○ With the **Zoom** tool selected, right-click the canvas to access more options. If you choose **Magnification**, **100%** you will go back to the original size. Another useful option is **Fit All**, to make the image exactly fill the window.

The Eyedropper tool

 ○ Click the **Eyedropper** tool in the **Tools** panel. This tool will allow you to sample colours on your canvas. Click on a colour in the canvas to sample it, then click the **Brush** tool and paint – hey presto! You can change the stroke or fill colour, depending on which of these is selected in the **Colors** section.

 ○ Select a fill colour and use the **Paint Bucket** tool to fill the area with this colour.

> **Tip**: When you are using the **Brush** or **Paint Bucket**, you can press and hold the **Alt** key to quickly bring up the **Eyedropper** tool. When you release the **Alt** key, the original drawing tool is automatically reselected.

Undoing mistakes

If you don't like the last line you painted, you can undo it by going to the **Menu** bar and selecting **Edit**, **Undo Brush** tool, or you can press **Ctrl-Z**.

You can undo a lot of strokes using **Window**, **History** (**Shift-F10**). The **History** panel will appear in the **Panel** dock, and by using the slider on the left you can undo and redo several actions. Watch the results on the canvas as you slide.

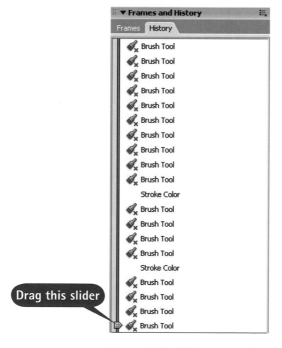

Figure 2.9: History panel

◗   Save your first piece as **test1.png** in your **Exercises** folder and close it.

Figure 2.10: Brush test

◗   Using your new knowledge, make some new canvases (**1000** pixels by **750**) and draw some pictures. Save them in your **Exercises** folder – you may be able to use them later!

Here are two that I created.

Figure 2.11: Sample pictures

Tip: You can change the colour of the canvas when you open a new file by clicking **Custom** and choosing a new background colour.

Maximising the workspace

A really good tip when working on a picture is to click the **Maximise** button in the top right of your canvas. This gives you a neutral border to paint across and when you zoom in, it shows you the maximum amount of picture on screen.

Maximise
will fill the screen with the canvas and a border. Click this button again to restore it to its original size.

Minimise
will put the canvas onto the bottom of the screen.

Close
will close the canvas. It will ask if you would like to save your picture first.

Figure 2.12: The Minimise, Maximise and Close buttons; these will be grey if the workspace is already maximised

Printing

◉ From the **Menu** bar, select **File**, **Page Setup**.

◉ Choose your printer's **Paper Size** and set the **Orientation** of the picture to **Landscape**.

◉ Press **OK** to confirm the changes.

Figure 2.13: The Page Setup dialogue box

○ From the **File** menu select **Print**. The dialogue box is shown below.

Figure 2.14: The Print dialogue box

○ You can now choose how many copies you want and click **OK** to print your favourite picture.

○ Select **File**, **Close** or click the **Close** button in the top right-hand corner of the canvas to close the picture.

○ Close Fireworks by clicking the **Close** button in the top right-hand corner of the window.

Selections

3

Making selections

A selection masks off an area so that you can paint it, move it, copy it or fill it with special effects.

There are three basic tools for making bitmap selections, as shown below.

 The **Marquee** tool (Rectangular or Oval)

 The **Magic Wand** tool

 The **Lasso** tool

The Marquee tool

The **Marquee** tool enables you to make selections using either a rectangle or an oval (ellipse). Let's try them out.

- ◉ Create a new canvas with a **Width** of **500 Pixels**, a **Height** of **500 Pixels**, a **Resolution** of **72 Pixels/Inch** and the **Canvas color** set to **White**.

 ◉ Click the **Rectangular Marquee** tool.

- ◉ The **Properties inspector** for the **Marquee** tool may already be open. If it is not, click **Window** on the **Menu** bar and then click **Properties**.

Drawing with the Marquee tool

- ◉ Set your options to match Figure 3.1.

Figure 3.1: Marquee tool options

▶ Click on the canvas and draw out a rectangle (see Figure 3.3). The rectangle expands from the start point as you drag.

▶ Draw a second rectangle and you will see that the first one disappears. You can click and drag inside the rectangle to move the selection.

 ▶ Select the **Paint Bucket** tool. Select a yellow colour and check the settings are as shown in Figure 3.2.

Figure 3.2: Paint Bucket tool options

▶ Click in the selected rectangle – the area floods with yellow. Deselect the rectangle by clicking **Ctrl-D**.

▶ Now click and hold the **Marquee** tool again and select the **Oval Marquee** tool option.

▶ Set the **Edge** option in the **Properties inspector** to **Anti-Alias**. This will smooth the rounded selection.

▶ Drag out a circle by holding down the **Shift** key after you have started drawing. (This technique can also be used to draw a square instead of a rectangle.)

Tip: You can also draw a rectangle or an ellipse with a fixed aspect ratio (width to height ratio) by changing the **Style** properties.

 ▶ Use a large **Brush** tool, say **50** pixels, with opacity set to **30** to fill the circle roughly with blue. Keep clicking and releasing the mouse button to add layers of paint (see Figure 3.3).

Figure 3.3: Selecting and filling shapes

Note: The black and white border around a selection is called a **marquee**. Sometimes it is referred to as the **marching ants**.

Moving a selection

Your blue circle should still be selected.

○ From the top of the **Tools** panel select the **Pointer** tool.

○ Click in the blue circle (the icon shows a pair of scissors, as you are cutting out the circle) and drag the circle across the yellow rectangle. The blue circle, with its patchy colouring, is moved.

○ Click **Ctrl–Z** to undo the move, then click on the **Subselection** tool.

○ Click in the blue circle and move it. Right away you will see that the icon has changed to a double arrow: this signifies you are dragging a copy of the blue circle.

Figure 3.4: Dragging a copied selection

Tip: Press **Shift** to constrain the angles or proportion of the move.

Transforming a selection

◐   With your copied circle still selected, choose **Modify**, **Transform**, **Free Transform** from the **Menu** bar. A box, called a **Transform box**, appears around the circle.

The little boxes around the edge of the **Transform box** are called **nodes**. See what happens when you place the mouse pointer over the nodes: the arrows show you the direction in which you can stretch, resize or even spin the circle.

◐   Pull, stretch, resize and spin your selection. When you have finished experimenting, press **Enter**.

◐   Press **Ctrl-D** to deselect.

Figure 3.5: Transforming a selection

Tip: You can complete the transformation in a few different ways: press **Enter**, double-click inside the transformation box, or click on another tool.

You will notice that you can see through bits of the blue circle. This is because the canvas is not part of your picture: imagine your shapes are floating above the white background. This feature is useful, but you will need to remember that if you change the canvas colour it can be a very dramatic change.

◐   Go to the **Menu** bar and choose **Modify**, **Canvas**, **Canvas Color**.

◐   In the dialogue box that pops up, choose **Custom** and pick **black** from the pop-up window.

◐   Press **OK**. The canvas colour changes to black – a big change!

Figure 3.6: Changing the canvas colour

The Magic Wand tool

You can use the **Magic Wand** tool to select an area of a particular colour. You can set the **Tolerance** level so that colours which are almost but not quite the same will be selected.

The **Magic Wand** tool will only work with overlapping shapes if they are on the same layer (we will discuss layers in detail in Chapter 5). For now, we will just merge all of the layers into one.

○ Press **Ctrl-A** to select all of the drawing objects, then, from the **Menu** bar, choose **Modify**, **Flatten Selection** (it's OK if this isn't available – it just means that everything is already on the same layer).

 ○ Click the **Magic Wand** tool and then click in the yellow rectangle.

The portion of the rectangle not overlapped by the circle will be selected.

Figure 3.7: Selecting with the Magic Wand tool

Setting the Tolerance level

You could select the ellipse in Figure 3.7 using the **Pointer** tool, but we will experiment with setting the **Tolerance** level of the **Magic Wand**.

○ In the **Properties inspector** for the **Magic Wand**, set the **Tolerance** to **10**.

○ Click in the old blue circle. Probably only a small portion of it will be selected.

○ Keep increasing the **Tolerance** until the whole circle is selected.

○ Use the shortcut **Ctrl-D** to deselect.

Adding and subtracting selections

You add to selections by keeping the **Shift** key pressed while you make another selection.

○ Experiment with this technique, selecting the circle and the part of the rectangle that isn't overlapped.

○ You can close this image without saving – that's enough practice!

The Lasso tool

Let's test some of our new skills by drawing a pattern of flowers using the **Selection** and **Brush** tools.

◗   Open a new canvas and specify a **Custom** green background.

◗   Select the **Lasso** tool. By dragging the mouse pointer, draw a flower shape, as shown in Figure 3.8.

Tip: Don't forget you can have as many goes as you like to get it right. Just use the shortcut **Ctrl-D** to deselect, or click **Select** on the **Menu** bar and click on **Deselect**. This will deselect the flower so you can draw another flower shape.

Figure 3.8: Flower selection

◗   Now select the **Paint Bucket** tool. Choose a white **Fill** colour. Move the mouse pointer over to the canvas, click and colour in the petals.

◗   Press **Ctrl-D**. You can now draw the next part of your picture.

◗   In the **Tools** panel, click on the **Marquee** tool and select the **Oval Marquee** tool.

◗   Draw a circle in the middle of the flower (remember to hold down **Shift**). You can use the arrow keys on the keyboard to nudge the selection into the perfect position, or you can drag the circle. Click the **Brush** tool and paint yellow in the circle selection (make sure the **Opacity** is set to **100**). Deselect when you have finished colouring.

Figure 3.9: Flower

You should have a flower that looks something like this! Now we are going to select the daisy and duplicate it all over the canvas.

Pasting daisies

○ Click the **Magic Wand** tool and select the yellow centre.

○ Keep **Shift** held down while you click in the white part of the flower to select it. You may have to click in several petals if your yellow circle overlaps them.

○ Press **Ctrl** and **Alt** together, then click inside your selection and drag a duplicate of the flower onto the green canvas. Release the mouse, then click and drag again several times to arrange the flowers on the canvas.

Tip: Remember you can click **Ctrl-Z** to undo as many actions as you want!

Figure 3.10: Lots of daisies

▷   Save your picture as **Daisies.png**.

You can use the **Magic Wand** tool to change the background colour. Then you can paint some shadows under the daisies using a soft brush, a slightly darker shade and a low opacity.

▷   Try creating some other masterpieces!

Figure 3.11: Variations on a theme

Cloning

4

Cloning

The **Rubber Stamp** tool is very powerful and is one of the most frequently used implements in the world of professional photo retouchers and computer artists. You'll need to spend some time playing around with it to understand how it works.

▷ Create a new canvas with a **Width** of **500 Pixels**, a **Height** of **500 Pixels**, a **Resolution** of **72 Pixels/Inch** and choose a **Custom** purple canvas colour.

We are going to make a cartoon of a pig's face, something like the one in Figure 4.1.

Figure 4.1: Creating your cartoon

Let's start with the pig's eyes.

▷ In the **Tools** panel, click the **Oval Marquee** tool and draw an oval roughly where I have drawn the pig's left eye.

▷ Choose a soft-edged **Brush** tool and set the brush size to **100**, opacity **100%**. (**Opacity** determines how 'thickly' the paint is laid on. The higher the opacity, the thicker the paint.)

▶ Paint the eye white.

Now we need a purple slightly darker than the background.

▶ Choose the **Eyedropper** tool and click the purple background.

▶ Now select the **Brush** tool and you will notice the **Properties inspector** shows the purple colour. Click on the **Color** box (see Figure 4.2).

▶ Click the **Sys color picker** to bring up the **Color pop-up** window. On the right-hand side, slide the bar down to darken your colour and then click **OK**.

Figure 4.2: Selecting your colour

▶ Reduce the size of the **Brush** tool to **60** and carefully spray a shadow area at the bottom of the eye. I would set the **Opacity** to **10** before you start to spray the shadow, so you can build up the colour without overdoing it.

▶ Deselect (**Ctrl–D**) and draw a circle selection to make the pupil. Colour it black and think about where you are placing it because you could make a big difference in the character's expression.

▶ Spray a white highlight over the pupil to give it a sparkle. Make the brush size **30** and the opacity **100%**, and just give it one burst of highlight.

Figure 4.3: Eye eye!

Tip: Remember that you can press **Ctrl-Z** or select **Edit**, **Undo** from the menu to undo an action and try again.

Using the Rubber Stamp tool

You can use the **Rubber Stamp** tool to paint an exact copy of any part of an image.

Once you have selected the **Rubber Stamp** tool, there are three stages to using it.

1. Set the **Properties**.

2. Activate the **Rubber Stamp** tool by pressing the **Alt** key, moving the crosshair over the area you want to clone (in this case the eye) and clicking.

3. Move the circle cursor to the area you want your **Rubber Stamp** tool to paint and click to paint.

Now give it a try, following the instructions below.

▶ Press **Ctrl-D** to make sure that nothing is selected.

 ▶ Click the **Rubber Stamp** tool and set the **Tool Properties** as shown in Figure 4.4.

Figure 4.4: Rubber Stamp properties

▶ Press and hold the **Alt** key and click somewhere in the pig's eye to activate the **Rubber Stamp** tool. Release the **Alt** key again.

▶ Move the mouse pointer to the position you want to **Rubber Stamp** a new eye! If the eye is in the wrong position this will give you a chance to practise moving a selection.

▶ Start painting in small circles to clone the eye.

Figure 4.5: Starting to Rubber Stamp the eye

▶ Finish cloning the eye.

Moving a selection

The eye in Figure 4.5 is too high and needs to be moved.

When the whole eye is selected, the **Marquee** tool changes shape to that of the **Marquee Move** tool as it passes over the selection.

Try it as follows.

 ● Use the **Magic Wand** to select the white part of the right eye. Then hold down **Shift** while you select the pupil.

> **Tip**: Don't forget, you can change the magic wand tolerance so you can more easily select the gradients.

 ● Now click the **Pointer** tool (or press **Ctrl** and the arrow keys) and move the eye. You should see something like Figure 4.6.

Figure 4.6: Moving a selection

It is quite usual to find that the **Magic Wand** misses some of the selection, so that a trace of the object is left in the original position. We can fix that now.

● From the **Select** menu, choose **Select Inverse**.

 ● Using the **Eraser** tool, carefully erase the left-over bits.

● Deselect by pressing **Ctrl–D**.

Subtracting selections

You already know how to add selections by holding down **Shift** as you make a second or third selection. You can also subtract portions of a selection by holding down the **Alt** key.

Let's paint the mouth using this technique.

● Click the **Oval Marquee** tool and draw a large oval selection (see Figure 4.7).

● Now hold the **Alt** key down and draw another oval starting from near the left eye.

The second oval has eaten away at the first oval, giving us a neat mouth shape.

▶ You can drag the selection, or use the arrow keys to move the selection if you need to.

Figure 4.7: Subtracting selections

Note: You will probably need several goes to get a shape you like. It is worth the effort.

▶ Use the **Brush** tool to spray the mouth dark purple and, decreasing the **Opacity** to about **20**, spray a small amount of the canvas colour on the bottom lip.

Tip: When you airbrush fine gradients, build them up in fine layers and you will get a much better result.

Modifying a selection

Sometimes the selection area is almost, but not quite, what you want. You can modify it.

▶ From the **Select** menu, choose **Contract Marquee**. Set the **Contract Marquee** window to **10** pixels and press **OK**. You should see that the selection has become smaller.

▶ Go back to **Select** and this time go to **Feather**. Set the **Feather Radius** to **4** pixels and press **OK**. This will give a soft edge to the selection.

▶ Colour the selection so that it looks something like Figure 4.8.

Figure 4.8: A contracted, feathered selection (note the soft edge to the mouth)

 ▶ Now select the **Lasso** tool and, holding down the **Alt** key, cut out some tombstone teeth like the ones in Figure 4.9.

Figure 4.9: Cutting out the teeth

▶ With the **Brush**, paint the teeth a grimy colour. You can use the **Sys color picker** and the pop-up **Color** window to get a really bad tooth colour.

▶ Use the **Oval Marquee** tool to draw the pig's nose and then drag the selection to place it slightly over the right eye. Colour it a lighter purple than the background.

▶ Look at Figure 4.10. Create the right nostril using a circle or ellipse and carefully spray black around the top of it.

▶ We need another nostril, so use the **Rubber Stamp** tool again.

Figure 4.10: Adding the nostrils

If you look at Figure 4.11, you will see I have made the pig slightly 3-D on the face by spraying lighter purple above the nose and dark purple under it.

 ● Click the **Magic Wand** tool and, with the **Tolerance** set very low, select the purple background.

 ● With the **Brush** tool set to size **100** and **Opacity 15%**, spray light purple above the nose and dark purple under it.

Finishing touches

You can use the **Lasso** tool to add the ears, some manic eyebrows in black and, last, some hair.

Figure 4.11: Mad Pig

● Save your cartoon as **MadPig.png** in your **Exercises** folder.

Working with Layers

Layers are like transparent sheets arranged on top of each other. They can be arranged in different orders and switched on and off. You can even make the layers react to different colours or contrasts and blend together to make some spectacular pictures.

Layers enable you to work on one element of your picture without changing the other elements and without having to make selections.

Figure 5.1: Layers

◉   Create a new canvas with a **Width** of **600 Pixels**, a **Height** of **700 Pixels**, a **Resolution** of **72 Pixels/Inch** and the **Canvas color** set to **White**.

◉   Look at the **Layers** panel on the right of your screen. It should look like Figure 5.2.

Figure 5.2: Layers panel

The top layer in the **Layers** panel is always the **Web** layer. This contains web objects such as **hotspots**, **slices** and **rollovers**. When you create any of these objects in any layer, they are automatically placed in the **Web** layer. You will try this out in Chapter 17.

The current layer name (**Layer 1**) is coloured blue in the **Layers** panel.

You need to be able to see the whole canvas.

◉ Select **View, Fit All** from the **Menu** bar.

Before you can paint the canvas, you have to insert a new bitmap image on the current layer.

 ◉ Click the **New Bitmap Image** icon at the bottom of the **Layers** panel (see Figure 5.2). Notice the new bitmap object appears under **Layer 1**.

 ◉ Click and hold the **Paint Bucket** tool. Select the **Gradient** tool and match the **Gradient** tool **Properties inspector** to Figure 5.3. (The **Texture** box can be set to anything, as no texture will be applied if the box next to it is set to zero.)

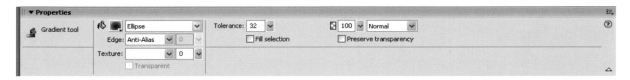

Figure 5.3: Paint bucket options

◉ Click the **Fill color** box and select **Preset: Blue, Red, Yellow**.

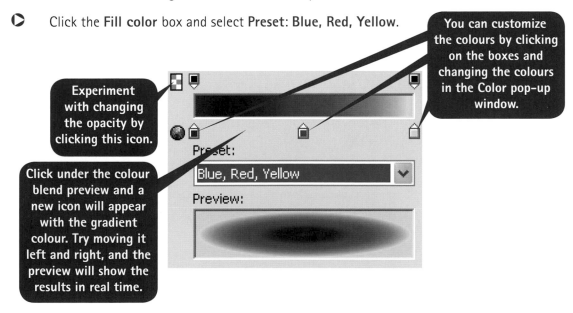

Figure 5.4: Colour gradients

◉ Click in the canvas – you should see a gradient pattern like Figure 5.5.

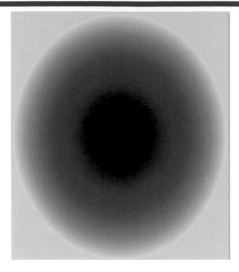

Figure 5.5: Gradient

Naming layers

It is a good idea to rename your layers as you go, so that you know at a glance what is on each layer.

○ Double-click on the name **Layer 1** in the **Layers** panel. Rename the layer **GradientBackground**.

○ Save your picture as **Layers.png** in your **Exercises** folder.

Making a new layer

 ○ Click the **Options** icon at the top right of the **Layers** panel and from the pop-up menu choose **New Layer**.

○ In the **New Layer** dialogue box, enter **Rectangles** as the layer name and then click **OK**.

Figure 5.6: The New Layer dialogue box

Look at Figure 5.7 for what you should see in the **Layers** panel.

Figure 5.7: The Layers panel

Labels in Figure 5.7:
- Decreasing Opacity will make your layer transparent.
- The selected layer is highlighted in blue and a Pencil icon is shown here.
- Click the Eye to hide the layer.
- Options icon
- Blend options
- This is your new layer.
- The background layer.
- Drag a layer onto the trashcan to dump it.

○ Select the **Rectangles** layer by clicking on it (it will be coloured blue when selected).

○ With the **Rectangles** layer selected, pick the **Rectangular Marquee** tool and draw a rectangle. Keep the **Shift** key pressed down while you draw a complex criss-cross pattern of boxes. In the **Layers** panel, you will see the new **Bitmap** object appear in the **Rectangles** layer.

○ Select the **Paint Bucket** tool and change the **Fill Category** in the **Properties inspector** from **Ellipse** to **Solid**.

○ Pour a colour that really clashes with the background. The **Layers** panel will show what is on the **Rectangles** layer.

Figure 5.8: The Rectangles layer in the Layers panel

○ Press **Ctrl-D** to deselect.

Figure 5.9: Filled pattern

 ○ Make a new layer. You can do it a different way this time, by pressing the **New/Duplicate layer** icon at the bottom of the **Layers** panel.

○ If you have renamed the other two layers, the new layer will be called **Layer 1**. Double-click its name in the **Layers** panel and change its name to **BlackCircle**.

○ Make sure **BlackCircle** is selected in the **Layers** panel.

 ○ Click the **New Bitmap Image** button at the bottom of the **Layers** panel. If you forget to do this, you will automatically start drawing on one of the other layers.

○ Select the **Oval Marquee** tool and hold down the **Shift** key while you draw a large circle right in the middle of the canvas. Colour it black with the **Paint Bucket** tool.

○ Press **Ctrl-D** to deselect.

Understanding layers

Now experiment with these three layers to gain an understanding of how they work.

The different layers in your canvas appear in the same order as the names in the **Layers** panel.

○ Drag the layers so that they appear in the order **Rectangles**, **BlackCircle**, **GradientBackground**.

The black circle is now under the criss-cross pattern. If you were to put it under **GradientBackground** it would be completely covered.

 ○ Click the **Eye** icon and switch off and on all the layers.

Note: In this exercise, there is only one object in each layer, so it makes no difference whether you switch off the **Bitmap** object, or the whole layer. Switching off the layer automatically switches off every object in that layer.

With all the layers switched off, all you can see is the white canvas colour. As you have made your own background to cover the canvas, it would not make any difference to the final image if you had a transparent background. You can try this.

◉ From the **Menu** bar, select **Modify**, **Canvas**, **Canvas Color** and choose **Transparent**. You will notice that Fireworks shows a chequer-board pattern to show nothing is there.

Manipulating images on different layers

◉ With the **BlackCircle** layer selected, pick the **Pointer** tool and move the circle anywhere you like. Try moving **Rectangles** as well – you will see that each layer can be moved or shuffled in any order you like.

◉ Now use the **Opacity** slider in the **Layers** panel and experiment with the layers. Set them back to **100** when you are finished.

Figure 5.10: Layer opacity

◉ Experiment with the **Blend mode**, currently set to **Normal**.

I set the **Blend mode** for **Rectangles** to **Difference** and that for **BlackCircle** to **Hue**.

Figure 5.11: Blend modes

Figure 5.12: Some different effects

Try making some other funky backgrounds!

▶   Save your pictures as **Layers2.png**, **Layers3.png** and so on, in your **Exercises** folder.

Vector Graphics 6

Raster or bitmap images are made up from a grid of coloured pixels. The resolution of a picture is typically measured in pixels per inch (ppi – on-screen) or dots per inch (dpi – on paper). The more pixels per inch, the finer the detail in the picture. Raster images are very good for storing and changing photographic pictures, but if you enlarge the image the results will probably not be satisfactory and individual pixels will be visible.

Vector images are made from mathematical information about the curves, sizes and point positions, and colours. Whenever you change the size of a vector image, rotate it or skew the image, it is redrawn and will be perfect. This type of image is good for graphical shapes or text.

We are now going to create a vector image that can be used at any size in a variety of printed materials, such as a brochure, birthday card, postcard or poster as well as on a website.

You will need a mascot to add a bit of fun to the activity club marketing materials, so meet Base Camp Bunny!

Starting the vector rabbit

▶ Create a new canvas with a **Width** of **600 Pixels**, a **Height** of **800 Pixels**, a **Resolution** of **72 Pixels/Inch** and the **Canvas color** set to a **Custom** very light grey.

▶ Locate the **Vector** tool section in the **Tools** panel. Select the **Ellipse** tool. (It is on the same button as the vector **Rectangle** tool.)

○ Have a look in the **Properties inspector** shown in Figure 6.1. You will notice it has **Fill** (**Paint Bucket** tool) and **Stroke** (**Pencil** tool) colour boxes.

Figure 6.1: Vector properties

○ Click in the **Fill color** box and choose medium grey, **#999999**: this will now be the colour inside the vector shape.

○ Leave the **Stroke** colour as **Transparent**. This means there will be no pencil line around the shape we are about to draw.

○ Click and drag an ellipse on the canvas.

You can adjust, move and rotate the vector ellipse in several different ways.

○ If you click on the **Pointer** tool, you can move the ellipse. Now click on the **Subselection** tool next to it and you will be able to click and move any of the four nodes.

○ Undo your changes by using **Ctrl-Z**, or delete the ellipse and draw another one. This time, from the **Menu** bar select **Modify**, **Transform**, **Free Transform**. You can now move, resize and rotate the ellipse in any way.

○ Try to match Figure 6.2 and then press **Enter** or double-click to finish.

Each time you draw a shape, Fireworks will automatically place the new object in the layer.

Figure 6.2: Story so far!

◐ The ellipse has a pale blue line around it to show that it is selected. Press **Ctrl–D** to deselect.

When you pass the mouse pointer over the ellipse, a red line appears around the ellipse to show that it is a vector shape but is not currently selected. Try reselecting it with the **Pointer** tool and then deselecting again.

The ellipse you have just drawn will be the rabbit's head. We are going to add his eyes next.

◐ Draw a nice big white eye, as shown in Figure 6.3.

◐ Position it with the **Pointer** tool, if necessary.

◐ Hold down **Ctrl** and **Alt** while you drag to duplicate the eye. If you also press the **Shift** key this will lock the duplicated shape in a horizontal or vertical plane.

◐ Draw another ellipse with a black fill to make the pupil in the eye and duplicate it to the other eye.

Now for the cheeks.

◐ Draw a white ellipse, duplicate it and move it over a bit, so that it overlaps the first ellipse. Note that you are creating a new object called **Path** in **Layer 1** with each shape.

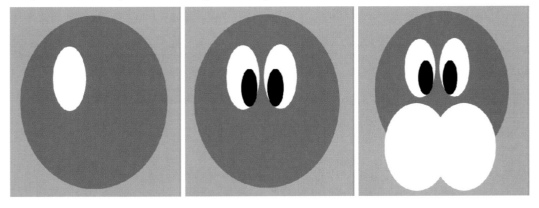

Figure 6.3: Building the bunny in stages

We can make these two ellipses into a single shape.

◐ Click the **Pointer** tool and keep the **Shift** key pressed while you select the first ellipse, so that both ellipses are selected.

◐ From the **Menu** bar, select **Modify**, **Combine Paths**, **Union**. The two cheeks combine to form a single vector shape or **Path**.

◐ Now that the cheeks are one vector shape, see if you can copy this shape, make it smaller, colour it pink and move it into position to make part of the nose, as shown in Figure 6.4.

◐ Draw a red circle to finish the nose.

Figure 6.4: Combined paths

◉ Draw another ellipse and colour it purple. It needs to be underneath the cheeks, so look in the **Layers** panel and drag the object (**Path**) down under the pink-coloured nose. Look at Figure 6.5 for inspiration!

 ◉ Use the **Rounded Rectangle** tool (on the same button as the vector **Ellipse** tool) to make some light yellow teeth and then rotate them slightly to make them look more 'buck'. Move the teeth layers between the pink nose layer and the purple mouth layer.

Figure 6.5: Buck teeth

Naming layers

Your **Layers** panel probably looks something like Figure 6.6 at this stage. By default, Fireworks gives names like **Path** or **Rounded Rectangle** to each vector object. (Bitmap objects are named **Bitmap** by default.)

Figure 6.6: The Layers panel

It is a good idea to rename the objects to indicate what is on each layer. Double-click the layer name to do this.

Figure 6.7: Renaming the objects in the Layers panel

- ▶ Before we complete the last bit, you can resize and reposition the drawing. First, select the whole image by dragging around it with the **Pointer** tool.

- ▶ Then select **Modify**, **Transform**, **Free Transform** (or use the shortcut **Ctrl-T**) to make the rabbit's head about half the canvas height and position it near the bottom of the canvas.

Copying and pasting objects

Now we need to draw the ears.

- ▶ Draw and position the first ear shape as a rotated ellipse (see Figure 6.8).

- ▶ To get the same colour you used for the face, click the **Fill color** box and move the mouse pointer over the rabbit so that the mouse pointer changes into an **Eyedropper** tool. Click on the medium grey of the rabbit's head.

- ▶ Select the **Pointer** tool, click the ear shape and from the **Menu** bar select **Edit**, **Copy** (or press **Ctrl-C**).

- ▶ Now select **Edit**, **Paste** (or press **Ctrl-V**).

- ▶ The pasted copy will appear on top of the first ellipse. Click and drag it to its new position and rotate it using **Modify**, **Transform**, **Free Transform**.

Tip: If your ears cover the eyes, drag the layers all the way to the bottom. Or you could use **Modify, Arrange, Send to Back**.

Figure 6.8: Ear we go!

○ Make two pink ellipses to put inside the ears (see Figure 6.9).

○ Use the **Subselection** tool to customise the insides of the ears. Click the ellipse with the Subselection tool, click the bottom node (it will turn blue) and drag it up to flatten the bottom of the ellipse.

○ Make a droopy ear with another ellipse the same colour as the ears, making sure it goes over the top of the pink ear pieces.

○ Use the vector **Line** tool to add some whiskers.

Figure 6.9: Base Camp Bunny

You will probably find that some of your objects are not quite correctly positioned.

○ Use the **Pointer** tool to select an object that you want to move, or right-click and choose **Transform**, **Scale** to make bigger changes.

Remember that you can select several shapes at once by holding down **Shift** while you select each one.

○ Save your vector artwork as **BaseCampBunny.png** in your **Components** folder.

Layer styles

Right, let's add some fantastic **filters** – these can transform your vector illustration in moments.

▶ Start by selecting the round nose by clicking on it with the **Pointer** tool.

▶ Find **Filters** at the bottom right of the **Properties inspector**.

▶ Click the + sign; choose **Shadow and Glow**, **Drop Shadow** and choose settings as shown in Figure 6.10. The changes will be applied as you change the settings.

Figure 6.10: Drop shadow options

▶ Click on the canvas to apply the drop shadow.

▶ Click the + sign to add another filter: **Eye Candy 4000 LE**, **Bevel Boss**.

▶ Match the settings to Figure 6.11. Click the **Lighting** and **Bevel Profile** tabs and experiment until you get a really rounded shiny nose! Press **OK** to apply the changes.

Tip: The lighting angle controls the light source direction. The bevel profile will help give your object a real three-dimensional quality, so always adjust it to achieve the best possible effect.

Figure 6.11: Eye Candy nose!

▶ Click the other shapes and add drop shadows or a little bit of moulding to make the rabbit a bit more three-dimensional.

If you change your mind about a filter, you can turn it off temporarily or delete it altogether (see Figure 6.12).

Click the tick and your filter will be temporarily switched off – try it! Select a filter and click the – sign to delete the effect altogether.

Click on the i and the Options box will pop up so you can edit the filters.

Figure 6.12: Editing your filters

◑ Save your picture with a different name: **BaseCampBunny3d.png**.

Figure 6.13: Finished bunny

Enlarging or resizing

When you draw a shape, or write some text using the **Text** tool, the shapes and text are **vector** graphics. When you use the **Brush** tool to spray a bit of the canvas, this is a **bitmap** or **raster** image.

Vector images are independent of resolution; the computer remembers the geometrical information associated with that shape and if the resolution or image size is changed, the shape can simply be redrawn with no loss of image quality. The extra information that allows the software to do this is called embedded information.

Raster images, because they are stored as a collection of different-coloured pixels, will become pixilated if they are enlarged too much. This is why you should always enlarge a vector image to its final size before you turn it into a raster image, not after.

The **BaseCampBunny** is a **vector** image. The **MadPig** you created in Chapter 4 is a **raster** image. We'll look at what happens when we zoom in and resize each image.

○   Open your **BaseCampBunny.png** (which should have no effects applied to it) and your **MadPig.png** files. The two file names will appear on the tabs at the top of the canvas and you can click a tab to see the image.

○   **Zoom in** on both pictures in turn, as far as the zoom will go.

You will see both images have pixilated edges. This is because computer monitors display images on a grid made up of pixels, which means that although vector images should appear with perfectly smooth edges, the data is displayed as pixels on-screen.

Now see what happens when we make the canvas bigger.

○   Start with **MadPig**. Reset the picture to **100%** zoom – the magnification factor is shown in the blue **Title** bar (you can do this quickly by pressing **Ctrl-1**).

○   Select **Modify, Canvas, Image Size** from the **Menu** bar.

○   Copy the width and height settings from Figure 6.14. Click **OK**.

Figure 6.14: Image size settings for the raster image

The image has increased in size. Notice that the image is quite blurred. This is because, to show the **raster** image at this size, Fireworks divided up the existing pixels, since there is no further information stored in the image.

Figure 6.15: The raster image is blurred

◐   Now click on the **BaseCampBunny** image. Reset the picture to **100%** zoom.

◐   Select **Modify, Canvas, Image Size** from the **Menu** bar.

◐   Copy the settings from Figure 6.16.

Figure 6.16: Image size settings for the vector image

◐   Click **OK** and have a look.

Figure 6.17: The vector image is sharp after resizing

The edges are still sharp because the shape information embedded in the **vector** image has been used to re-draw the image at a larger size.

▶   Close both images without saving.

Tip: Use a word processor to make an entry in your **Elements** table for **BaseCampBunny**, which is from a primary source (since you created it).

We will be using the bunny in the birthday card and other artwork. It will be one of the recognisable symbols of the **Base Camp** activity club, along with the logo which you will develop in the next chapter. Using the same image over and over helps to create a recognisable brand.

Can you think of other companies which use a character or symbol as well as a logo?

Converting vector images into raster images

There are certain things you cannot do with **vector** graphics, which is why we sometimes need to simplify a layer, or **flatten** an image. Doing this turns it into a **raster** layer or **raster** image.

When you do this, the software remembers which colour is in which pixel, but it no longer knows where one shape ends and another one starts.

If you imagine a **vector** image being a pile of shapes that can be individually picked up and moved around, turning that **vector** image into a **raster** image is like taking a photo of all the shapes; the image looks the same, but now you cannot pick up and move the individual shapes.

Creating a Logo

You will need to do some background work before you start to design graphics components for Base Camp. All graphic designers and illustrators have huge libraries of source material; anything you see and like you should collect and store, so that you can browse through your collection when you are searching for inspiration. Your library of source material might take the form of a list of favourites in your web browser, or a folder containing graphics you have downloaded and information about where you found them.

> **Tip**: It is good practice to make a note in the **Elements** table of all the images you use or create (see Chapter 1, Figure 1.5, page 7).

Before you start to design the Base Camp logo, you need to ask yourself some questions.

- What it is for?
- Who it is for?
- How it is going to be used?
- What typeface would be appropriate?

For this exercise, you have to design a logo for an outdoor adventure centre called Base Camp. It should be designed to appeal to children aged between 9 and 14.

The logo will be used in different advertising materials, so it needs to be identifiable as outdoors based, and it needs to be bright and fun so that kids can relate to it. Also, a good logo can be used for T-shirts, stickers and mugs and can become a cool symbol of its brand. (You are probably wearing at least one item with a logo!)

Here are some tips for designing logos.

- Keep it simple.
- Do your research. Look at other company logos and decide what you like about them and what you don't like.
- Design in black and white initially.
- Make sure your company name is clear.
- Choose colours carefully.

▶ Choose typefaces carefully.

▶ Make sure they work in a variety of sizes.

▶ Pause to reflect, and come back to your logo in a week to see if you still like it. Check it for typos!

▶ Avoid clip art.

▶ Do a mock-up of your logo where it will be used (in documents, on signs, on a vehicle and so on) to see if it works.

Collecting secondary components

A word about copyright

There is a huge amount of material available on the web, and you should take advantage of it.

A lot of websites are happy for you to download free resources, provided they aren't for commercial use (that is, you aren't going to profit financially from using them). For example, if you are using resources for a school or college assignment, then there is no need to seek permission for each component used. If you decide to publish a book using these components, then clearly you must ask permission.

Copying images from other websites

The best way to search for images on a particular subject is to use a search engine. Google™ is particularly useful because it can search specifically for images.

Load your favourite browser (e.g. Microsoft® Internet Explorer), then go to the **Google**™ homepage (**www.google.co.uk**). Type the search criteria **Logo**, then click **Google Search**.

You'll find there are plenty of sites that give advice on developing logos.

Figure 7.1: An example of a Google™ splash page

- Now have a look at some sample logos: click where it says **Images** at the top of the screen.

- If you find a suitable image, click on it to visit the website it originates from. Right-click it and then select **Save Picture As** from the menu that appears.

- Save the picture in your **Logo\Reference** folder.

Designing the logo

I have found some logos on the Internet that I like and think will appeal to kids. I've looked at magazines for lovers of extreme sports such as snowboarding, mountain biking, mountaineering, kite surfing and canoeing.

The next stage is to start sketching logos. Most importantly, add your text. There are endless possible variations, but the rule of thumb is: 'If it looks right, it is right, and if it looks wrong, chuck it away and start again.' I have, on occasions, spent days trying to make something work only for the client to tell me what I already knew: 'It doesn't look right!'

- With pen and paper, start to sketch ideas.

Figure 7.2: My sketched ideas showing my thought processes

You will need to annotate your ideas and then scan them – or you can scan them, insert them in a word-processing document and then add annotations.

Scanning

Scanning is useful when you need an electronic copy of printed media such as a photo or hand-drawn image.

You can scan an image directly from Fireworks if your scanner is TWAIN compliant (Windows®). This is very convenient because you can also edit the scanned image using Fireworks to improve image quality and reduce the file size. To scan from Fireworks, do the following.

▶   Open Fireworks.

▶   Select **File**, **Scan**, **Twain Acquire** from the **Menu** bar. The next window will either be a list from which you need to select your scanner, or it will go directly to the scanner window (if you have scanned from Fireworks before).

Figure 7.3: Scanner options/preview window; this will look different for different scanners, but the same options will be available

Scanned file resolutions

The scanned document will be viewed only on-screen (not printed out), so it will be viewed at **72 pixels/inch** (or dpi). It is worth scanning at a slightly higher resolution than this to ensure the document is as clear as possible (e.g. use a scanning resolution of about **100 pixels/inch**).

Don't be tempted to use a higher resolution than is needed because it will take longer to scan, it will be a larger file and will require more optimisation later.

◉ Set the **Scan resolution** to **100dpi** and make sure it is set to **Color** if you are scanning a colour picture.

◉ Click the **Preview** button to preview what the scan will look like.

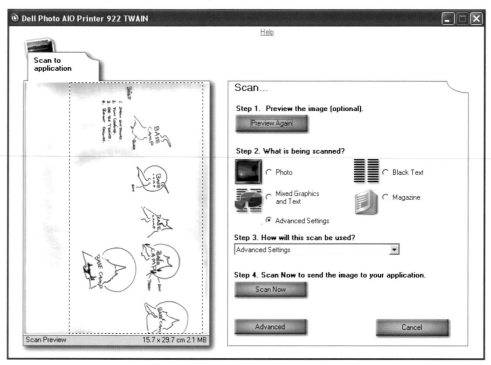

Figure 7.4: Previewing and cropping the scan

◉ If you need only a specific area of the document to be scanned, just click and drag the box in the **Scan Preview** area to surround the part that you want.

◉ Click **Scan** when you're ready.

The scan will take a minute or so, then the scanned document will appear in the Fireworks workspace.

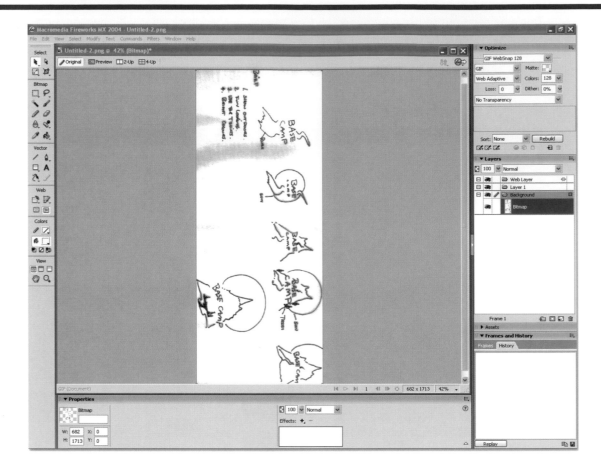

Figures 7.5: Completed scan

○ If you need to rotate the image, select **Modify**, **Canvas** from the **Menu** bar. Select a rotate option to suit.

○ If you need to resize the image, select **Modify**, **Canvas**, **Image Size** from the **Menu** bar. Select a width to suit. Press **OK** to apply the change.

○ Save the scanned document by selecting **File**, **Save As** from the **Menu** bar. If you are scanning a set of logo ideas, you should save it in your **Logo\Scans** folder. It will be saved as a **.png** file by default; this is fine, as you can save it as a **.jpg** or **.gif** file when you optimise it.

Creating the logo

○ Create a new canvas with a **Width** of **800 Pixels**, a **Height** of **800 Pixels**, a **Resolution** of **72 Pixels/Inch**, and the **Canvas color** set to **White**.

Using the Pen tool

We will draw the mountain first. You may need to find some pictures of mountains to use as a reference, as this has got to look good.

You will be using the vector **Pen** tool, which is a little tricky to master so you will need to spend time experimenting with it. Try a test shape first.

 ➲   Select the **Pen** tool and match the **Properties inspector** to Figure 7.6.

Figure 7.6: Pen tool settings

➲   First, try drawing a closed shape made up of straight lines. Simply click and release the mouse at several points roughly round a square, circle or other shape. When you hover near the first point, you will see a little circle appear to tell you that the next click will close the shape.

➲   Press the **Delete** key twice to delete your shape.

Now you're ready to try curves – this can be a little tricky at first!

➲   With the **Pen** tool still selected, click anywhere on the canvas.

➲   Now position the mouse pointer a short distance from where you have just clicked. This time, keep the left button pressed while you drag and then release. A neat curved path appears.

➲   Repeat. (Position the mouse pointer again a short distance away, then press and hold the left button while you drag and release again.) The beauty of drawing like this is that you can tweak the lines all you want at any stage of the design process.

Figure 7.7: Mastering the Pen tool

▶ Draw a wobbly line and go all the way back to your original point. Close the shape as before.

 ▶ In the **Properties inspector**, click on the **Fill color** box and choose a colour to fill your shape with.

▶ Try changing the colour in the **Stroke color** box now. You can even switch it off to leave just the filled shape.

▶ Click the **Subselection** tool, and click and drag a point on your shape to move it. You can also delete the selected point by pressing the **Delete** key.

Drawing the mountain shape

▶ That's enough experimenting! With the **Pointer** tool selected, click on your shape and delete it, as we are going to draw the mountain now.

 ▶ Select the **Pen** tool and make sure the **Properties inspector** looks like Figure 7.6.

▶ Draw the mountain shape using a combination of straight lines and curves. Use the **Subselection** tool to tweak it until you are happy with it. I took nine attempts before I liked mine.

Figure 7.8: The mountain shape

▶ Fill the mountain shape with blue. Look at the **Layers** panel – your mountain shape appears in **Layer 1** with the default name **Path**.

▶ Deselect the mountain by pressing **Crtl-D**.

Drawing the sun

 ▶ Choose the vector **Ellipse** tool and draw the sun, keeping the **Shift** key pressed to constrain its proportions.

▶ Fill the sun with a warm orangey-yellow and turn off its stroke colour.

◉ In the **Layers** panel, you can order the vector shapes by dragging their object names up or down.

Figure 7.9: Layers panel

◉ Drag the sun under the mountain in the **Layers** panel.

◉ Rename the two objects **Mountain** and **Sun**.

◉ Use **Modify, Transform, Free Transform** to size and position your circle.

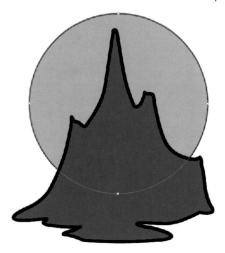

Figure 7.10: Mountain and sun

Snow-capped mountain

◉ Double-click the name **Layer 1** in the **Layers** panel and rename it **MountainAndSun**.

◉ Select just the **Mountain** object and then drag it onto the **New/Duplicate Layer** icon at the bottom of the **Layers** panel.

◉ This creates a duplicate of the mountain on a new layer called **Layer 1**. Rename the layer **Snowcap**.

◉ Switch off the **MountainAndSun** layer by clicking the **Eye** symbol in the **Layers** panel. Now all you can see is the duplicate **Mountain** object.

- Press **Ctrl-D** to deselect the **Mountain** object.

- Select the **Pen** tool and change the settings in the **Properties inspector** back to those shown in Figure 7.6.

- Draw a wobbly snowy line, as shown in Figure 7.11. The line needs to show the snowline near the mountain peak. Take the line around the outside of the mountain to close it.

> **Start here and work anti-clockwise, drawing the snowline first then going round the top to close the line.**

Figure 7.11: Adding a snowy peak

Next we will crop the snow cap to the exact shape of the mountain peak.

- With the **Pointer** tool, select the mountain. Press and hold the **Shift** key while you select the new wobbly line.

- From the **Menu** bar, select **Modify**, **Combine Paths**, **Crop**. We now have our snow shape!

- Change the **Fill** colour to white.

- Switch on the **MountainAndSun** layer.

Figure 7.12: The cropped snow cap

Lake and stream

◐ Now see if you can add a mountain lake and stream. You will need to make a new layer with the **Mountain** object on it, exactly as before, and name the layer **LakeAndStream**. Use the **Pen** tool to draw a lake and stream, and crop as before.

The final tweaks are up to you. Use the **Pointer** tool to select the separate shapes, then change the **Fill** colours and the **Stroke** sizes and colours to make a punchy image.

Figure 7.13: All coloured up!

Using the Text tool

Adding the text is the 'make-or-break' moment for this logo – you need to make sure it is readable, fun and looks good.

Your computer probably has many different typefaces, so spend some time exploring them.

When you select one, remember who the logo is designed to appeal to and what it will be used for.

First you need a new layer. This keeps your artwork neat and organised; when you are working on a much more complicated piece of artwork, this will be even more necessary!

◐ Click the **New/Duplicate Layer** icon.

◐ Rename the layer **TitleText**.

◐ Click on the **Text** tool in the **Vector** section of the **Tools** panel.

◐ In the **Properties inspector**, make sure the text is left-aligned and select a suitable font (**Comic Sans MS** will do) about size **60**, in a green colour.

Figure 7.14: The Text tool settings

- Click on the canvas. You will notice that Fireworks has made a new vector object called **Text** in the **TitleText** layer.

- Type **Base Camp**.

- To move the text you must first select it with the **Pointer** tool. Do this and then play with the colours and typefaces. You could try adding an effect or two. (Click the **+** sign next to **Filters**.)

- You could save two or three versions with different text styles. For now, choose the best version and we will finish off the logo.

Attaching text to a path

The logo probably looks OK at the moment, but we will give the text a curve to see if that makes it look even better.

- Draw a large vector **Ellipse**, and in the **Properties inspector** set the fill to **None** and make a **1** pixel **black** stroke.

- Press **Shift** and select the text.

- From the **Menu** bar, choose **Text**, **Attach to Path**.

Figure 7.15: Attaching text to a path

- Click the **Text** tool and click on the ellipse in front of the **Base Camp** text – you may need to add some spaces to centralise the text.

- Save this version of the logo and then add some tweaks and colour changes until it is perfect.

- Save the final version as **BaseCampLogo.png** in your **Logo\Artwork** folder.

Figure 7.16: The finished logo

Filters and Effects

You can create some spectacular results very quickly by adding different filters or effects to a picture. You can also transform a photograph into something quite different! We have already used effects such as drop shadows and a little bit of moulding on vector shapes.

In this chapter you will create a fancy button which you could use on your Base Camp web page. You'll also be adding special effects to two different photographs. These could be placed in your Base Camp web page, or used on postcards, birthday cards, brochures or posters.

Brushed steel button

- ○ Create a new canvas with a **Width** of **500 Pixels**, a **Height** of **500 Pixels**, a **Resolution** of **72 Pixels/Inch** and the **Canvas color** set to **Transparent**.

- ○ Click the **New Bitmap Image** icon at the bottom of the **Layers** panel; this will give you a transparent canvas to work on.

- ○ Select the **Paint Bucket** tool, choose a light grey and flood the canvas with the colour.

- ○ On the **Menu** bar, choose **Filters**, **Noise**, **Add Noise** and match the **Add Noise** dialogue box to the settings shown in Figure 8.1. Click **OK**.

Figure 8.1: Adding noise

- ○ Choose **Filters**, **Blur**, **Motion Blur** and match the direction and length of the blur to the settings shown in Figure 8.2: Angle **0** and Distance **38**. Click **OK**.

Figure 8.2: Motion Blur

There are several ways to do the next stage, but the method explained below is the best because it is the easiest to update.

 ● Select the **Oval Marquee** tool and check that the **Edge** property is set to **Anti-alias**.

● Draw a circle selection on the stainless steel background.

Figure 8.3: Selection

● From the **Menu** bar, choose **Select**, **Select Inverse** to select everything except the current selection. Press the **Delete** key to clear the unwanted background.

● Press **Ctrl-D** to deselect. In the **Layers** panel, rename this layer (**Layer 1**) as **Button**. (Double-click the layer name to do this.)

● Drag the **Button** layer down onto the **New/Duplicate Layer** icon to duplicate this layer.

● Rename the new layer **ButtonCopy**.

Click on the **Pointer** tool, which should automatically select the **ButtonCopy** layer. Click on your newly drawn button and, in the **Properties inspector**, click the **Add live filters** button and choose **Candy 4000 LE, Bevel Boss**.

Copy the **Basic** settings from Figure 8.4 and choose appropriate **Lighting** and **Bevel Profile** settings.

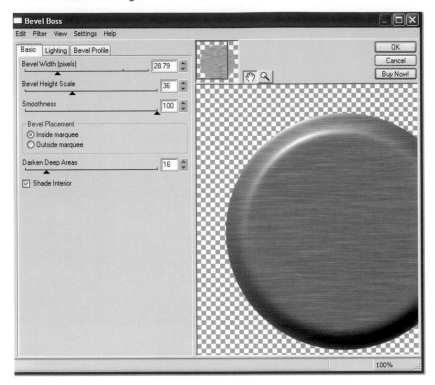

Figure 8.4: Bevel Boss

Click **OK**.

Find the vector shape **Arrow**. (It shares a spot in the **Tools** panel with the **Rectangle** tool and **Ellipse** tool.)

Figure 8.5: Vector tools

○ Draw an arrow onto the button. Have a play with the various nodes around the arrow path – the blue nodes change the size of the arrow and the yellow ones change the shape. Experiment and you will find there are a few surprises!

Figure 8.6: Adding the arrow

○ With the arrow still selected, use the **Properties inspector** to add a new filter by clicking the **Add live filters** button and this time choose **Adjust Color**, **Hue/Saturation**. Use the settings shown in Figure 8.7.

Figure 8.7: Hue/Saturation

○ The next bit is up to you! Add a **bevel** and a **drop shadow** filter, to make the arrow look as stylish as possible.

Lastly we need a shadow for the button itself, which we can make by using an effect.

○ Turn off the **Button Copy** layer to reveal the **Button** layer. We'll make this layer into the shadow. Select the circle and, from the **Menu** bar, select **Filters**, **Adjust Color**, **Brightness/Contrast**. Make your stainless steel go black and press **OK**.

○ You will notice that in the **Properties inspector** there is no option to switch off or change the filter, although it is not uncommon to have to do this!

○ Now go to **Filters**, **Blur**, **Gaussian Blur**. Set it to about **10** and press **OK**.

Switch the **Button Copy** layer on and marvel at your home-made drop shadow. Using the **Pointer** tool, move the **Button** layer to get the shadow in the perfect place, matching the shadow with the highlights on your arrow.

Now click again on the arrow. You can see all your **Filters** are still attached and if you want to tweak the colour just click on the **Edit and arrange live filters** button next to **Hue/Saturation** (see Figure 8.8).

Figure 8.8: Editing your filters

Save your button in your **Components** folder as **Button.png** and close the file.

Tip: Don't forget to make an entry for it in your **Elements** table (see page 7).

Tip: When you scale an image that has live filters, you will almost certainly need to update the settings.

Downloading photographs

For the next two exercises, you will need to download photographs from the Payne-Gallway website. You will find all the images you need for these exercises at: **www.payne–gallway.co.uk**. From the home page, select **Adult Beginner** in the left-hand menu. Select **Fireworks 8 Right from the Start** and choose **student resources**.

Save the images in your **DownloadedImages** folder.

Adding the Wow! factor

Most of my work involves making photographs better or more exciting; this is one brilliant way of giving some Wow! factor.

Experimenting with layer blend modes can occasionally bring up some neat accidents. It is impossible sometimes to sketch ideas before you try to make an artwork, so try to make sure you save versions of your artwork as you get closer to finishing it. Every time I make a step forwards or I see something I like, I save straightaway using the picture name followed by **V1**, **V2** and so on (for Version 1, Version 2). That way I can always go back to a previous version if the next hour's work doesn't turn out well.

◐   Load Fireworks if it is not already open.

◐   From the **Menu** bar, select **File**, **Open** and browse to find your **DownloadedImages** folder. Change the **Files of type** box to **JPEG**.

◐   Select the picture **CatamaranSailing.jpg** and click **Open**.

Figure 8.9: Loading a JPEG file

 ◐   Choose the **Oval Marquee** tool and in the **Properties inspector** check that the **Style** is **Normal** and **Edge** is set to **Feather 100**. Feathering the selection makes the edge blurred.

◐   Draw an oval selection around the sailors, as shown in Figure 8.10.

Figure 8.10: Feathered selection

○ You can see how your selection looks by using the **Paint Bucket** tool, setting the **Opacity** to **100** and choosing a colour to show up against the photo. Tick the **Fill selection** box. Click in the middle of the selection.

○ Press **Ctrl-Z** to undo the fill. You want to apply a filter to the outside of the selection, so go to the **Menu** bar and choose **Select**, **Select Inverse**.

○ Now select **Filters**, **Blur**, **Zoom Blur**. I decided to set the options at **Amount 30** and **Quality 80**. It might take a few moments to apply the filter, depending on the speed of your computer. Click **OK**.

○ Press **Ctrl-D** to deselect.

Figure 8.11: Zoooom!

Well, that certainly gives the picture Wow! factor. We can now add some spectacular colour changes by adding another effect.

- ◉ Save the picture in your **Exercises** folder.

- ◉ At the top right of the **Layers** panel, you will find the **Options** button – click it and choose **Duplicate layer**, click the **After current layer** button and then click **OK**.

- ◉ Hold **Shift** and select both of the layers. At the top of the **Layers** panel, change the **Blend modes** and experiment to see how different blends work to make some very stylish and some very bad results.

Figure 8.12: Layer Blend modes

- ◉ Add a **New Bitmap Image** and add some filled shapes, then use the blend options in the **Layers** panel to make a surreal coloured creation ... can you do better than mine?

Figure 8.13: Wow ... hand me a pair of sunglasses!

- ◉ Save your favourite version in your **Exercises** folder.

Background image

Sometimes a filtered photograph can be used as a background for text. You have to remember that the text needs to be legible, so the colours you use are very important if the message is to come across clearly.

A background that is basically black or dark grey looks cool and classy, and yellow or grey will look more sporty or can be used for a warning sign.

Consider whether your design needs to grab people's attention. If it does, what age group is it aimed at? Could you use an image of a famous footballer or pop group, or use shock tactics to get people to look and read? (This would not be applicable or desirable for the Base Camp brochure!)

I have used the techniques described in the next exercise several times. They can be used with photographic images that are not particularly crisp, as long as they have good colour contrast, so that the shapes can be clearly picked out.

○   Load the picture **CampSite.jpg** from your **DownloadedImages** folder.

Figure 8.14: Camp site © Acorn Adventure

At the bottom of the photograph there is a canoe and fire-fighting equipment.

○   Use the **Rubber Stamp** tool to clone some gravel and paint them out. Choose your brush size carefully. You might also want to drop the opacity down to **75**. (Look back at Chapter 4 if you can't remember how to use the **Rubber Stamp** tool.)

Figure 8.15: Gone!

As you can see in Figure 8.14, the photo is a bit blurred but has lots of contrast and you can try out a combination of effects that will work well with this image.

○ Pick the **Pointer** tool and click on the canvas. Click on the **Add live filters** button and select **Other**, **Find Edges**.

The image is not very usable like this, but something I like to try with my images is to invert them, so that black becomes white and vice versa.

○ Click on the **Add live filters** button and select **Adjust Color**, **Invert**.

Figure 8.16: Inverted, it looks like a pencil sketch!

Now we can colour it. We could use another layer with a colour and use a **Layer Blend mode** so that the camp site is visible too, but this time we will add another effect to change and customise the background.

○ Click the **Add live filters** button and go to **Adjust Color**, **Hue/Saturation**. Copy the settings from Figure 8.17 and make sure you tick the **Colorize** checkbox. Press **OK** to apply the change.

Figure 8.17: Settings for the colorized background

Figure 8.18: Coloured background

You could now add, say, white text to this coloured background.

Note: Remember that all you need to do is click the **Edit and arrange live filters** icon in the **Properties inspector** to update the image. The original picture is untouched and if you switch off all the filters you can see it.

◐   From the **Menu** bar, select **File**, **Save**.

A message will be displayed telling you that you must save this as a **PNG** file if you want to be able to edit it further.

Figure 8.19: Option to save as PNG file

◐   Click **Save Fireworks PNG**. Save the file in your **Exercises** folder.

◐   Close the file.

Using Text and Guides

In this chapter you will learn how to use a grid and guides so that you can accurately lay out a folded document, such as a brochure or birthday card. If you had to produce a brochure, you would probably use desktop publishing software, but you could use Fireworks to create some text headings and graphics to use in the brochure. These would then be reusable in future brochures.

We will take a closer look at how to create and edit text and the options you can use to change its appearance in different ways.

Laying out a grid

For the brochure, I chose the size of the canvas to be roughly A3 size, assuming that the finished brochure will be an A3 sheet folded in the middle.

> **Note**: 72dpi is not a sufficiently high resolution for printed material. Therefore, this is strictly a mock-up that will be viewed only on-screen.

⬤ Create a new canvas with a **Width** of **1200 Pixels**, a **Height** of **850 Pixels**, a **Resolution** of **72 Pixels/Inch** and the **Canvas color** set to **White**.

> **Tip**: You can calculate the physical size of the canvas in inches by dividing the number of pixels by the resolution in pixels/dots per inch. Therefore, this canvas will be 1200 ÷ 72 = 16.7 inches wide and 850 ÷ 72 = 11.8 inches tall, which is roughly the size of an A3 sheet in landscape orientation.

⬤ Go to **View** on the **Menu** bar, and choose **Grid**, **Show Grid**. The screen is now covered in squares, but the grid needs to be edited for our purposes.

⬤ Choose **View**, **Grid**, **Edit Grid**. We need the grid to fit perfectly; the canvas is 1200 by 850 pixels, so a grid of 50 × 50 pixels will do nicely. Copy the settings in Figure 9.1 and click **OK**.

Figure 9.1: Setting the grid

Note: Notice that **Snap to grid** is checked – this will ensure that objects are placed exactly on gridlines rather than just very close to them.

Next it will be useful to have rulers so you can find the middle of the canvas and pull out guides to mark out the layout.

◐ Select **View, Rulers**.

◐ Now select **View, Guides, Edit Guides**.

◐ Copy Figure 9.2 and choose a dark red colour for the guides. Click **OK** to apply the changes.

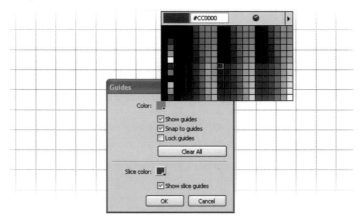

Figure 9.2: Editing the guides

Tip: If you are working on a dark canvas, you will need to choose light colours so you can see your grid and guides.

◐ Press **Ctrl-0** (that's **Ctrl** and **zero**, the shortcut key combination for **Fit All**). This will fit all of your canvas onto the screen.

◐ Click and hold on the left-hand ruler, drag a guide and measure along the top ruler **600 pixels**.

○   Look at Figure 9.3 and draw out guides so you have two pages marked out ready to design your brochure.

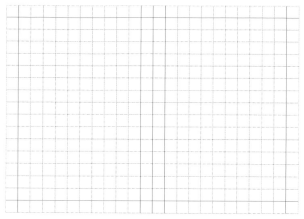

Figure 9.3: Grid and guides

Adding text

Next we will add some text and position it carefully.

 ○   Pick the **Text** tool and set the properties as shown in Figure 9.4. If you have not got the **Alba** font, choose something else.

Figure 9.4: Text properties

○   Click somewhere on the canvas. A small box will appear, as shown in Figure 9.5, and you can start typing.

Figure 9.5: Text box

○   Type: **BASE CAMP [Enter] The best fun you will ever have!**

○   Use the **Pointer** tool to position the text on the top left of the grid, and stretch the text box over to the right-hand guide.

Figure 9.6: Text moved into position

Editing text

You can edit and manipulate text in the **Text Editor** dialogue box.

> Display the **Text Editor** dialogue box. You can do this by selecting **Text**, **Editor** from the **Menu** bar, or by double-clicking the **Text** tool while your text box is selected.

Figure 9.7: Text editor

> Try selecting the title and making it much larger.

Scaling text

> Experiment with different typefaces. Try selecting the second line and clicking the **Stretched alignment** button so the text fits right across the text space. Click **OK** when you have finished.

Vertical text

Suppose you wanted to have vertical text down the left margin of the second page.

> Make sure nothing is currently selected.

○ Click the **Text** tool. In the **Properties inspector**, click the button to the left of the **Text alignment** buttons. Choose **Vertical left to right**.

Figure 9.8: Aligning the text

○ Type **Base Camp** on the second page.

Figure 9.9: Adding vertical text

○ Save your work as **BrochureInside.png** in your **Exercises** folder.

Combining text and effects

The next piece of artwork we will create will be a sign for Base Camp using a wood effect so that it looks as if the letters have been burnt onto a piece of wood. You will use Fireworks textured fills and effects to achieve this.

○ Create a new canvas with a **Width** of **500 Pixels**, a **Height** of **350 Pixels**, a **Resolution** of **72 Pixels/Inch** and the **Canvas color** set to **White**.

○ You may need to turn off the grid and guides if they are still switched on.

A   ◐   Select the **Text** tool and, in the **Properties inspector**, make sure that the **Stretch Alignment** button is not selected, that **text orientation** is set to **Horizontal left to right** and the text is centred. The colour is not important – leave it as green.

◐   Choose a typeface that suggests a home-made sign and enter a large font size, say **120**. (You will need to type in the font size, rather than using the slider, to get it big enough to nicely fill the whole canvas.)

◐   Click towards the middle of the canvas and type: **Base [Enter] Camp**.

◐   Use the **Pointer** tool to centre the text box in the canvas. Don't forget you can tweak the position with the arrow keys as well.

◐   With the **Pointer** tool or the **Text** tool selected, click the **Color** box in the **Properties inspector**, as we are going to explore the **Fill options**.

◐   Click **Fill Options** at the bottom of the **Color** pop-up window, find the **Fill category** at the top of the **Fill options** and change it to **Pattern**.

Figure 9.10: Pattern

◐   Click the **Pattern name** and scroll down to find **Wood**.

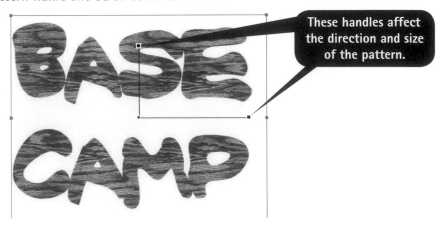

These handles affect the direction and size of the pattern.

Figure 9.11: Wood fill

This next bit is up to you. It will take a bit of work, so really try to achieve the right effect – the lettering has to appear as if it is engraved, or carved, into the background.

○ Add a **live filter** – you can use **Bevel and Emboss**, **Inset Emboss** or the **Eye Candy 4000 LE**, **Bevel Boss**.

○ With the vector **Rectangle** tool, draw a rectangle over the entire canvas. It should fill automatically with the **wood** pattern. If it does not, fill it using options in the **Properties inspector**.

○ In the **Layers** panel, drag the **Rectangle** object under the **Text** object.

○ Select the **Text** object.

○ Add another **live filter**. Select **Adjust Color**, **Hue/Saturation** and make the text look burnt by darkening it and taking a little colour saturation out – have a look at Figure 9.12 for reference.

Figure 9.12: Wood background

○ To add some realism, add one more **live filter**. Choose **Shadow and Glow**, **Glow**. Change the colour to a dark brown, then tweak the **Softness**, **Width** and **Opacity** to create a soft burnt effect around the letters.

Figure 9.13: Finished wood sign

○ Save your sign as **WoodSign.png** in your **Exercises** folder.

Birthday Card

If one of the Base Camp campers has a birthday, we need to have a card ready! Let's create a card using the Base Camp Bunny.

Making a mock-up of the card

Remember that this card is for kids, so it has to be bright and bold. It will have a front and back, and it will have some text inside.

I measured some birthday cards and found that 18 cm high and 14 cm wide (28 cm wide opened out) is a good average. This will fit on an A4 page, so it can be easily printed.

Think about where the front of the card will be when it is laid flat. It is a good idea to make a mock-up of the card, to make sure you don't mess up. A trip to an advertising agency will reveal mock-ups of all sorts of products in cardboard or paper form. Even the professionals need to look at and handle a physical object – quite often this will spark an idea or two. At the very least, it will help them to understand what they are dealing with.

▶   Roughly measure and cut out a card using my measurements.

▶   Sketch the rabbit head on the front of the card and add a birthday message inside.

▶   Take a digital photo of your mock-up card standing up. Save your photograph in your **BirthdayCard\Development** folder.

Figure 10.1: My card

Modifying the canvas size

○ Open **BaseCampBunny3d.png**.

○ Save the file as **RabbitCardV1** in **BirthdayCard\Artwork**.

We will create the card artwork at 72dpi (screen resolution). As it will be vector art, we can enlarge it for print later without affecting the quality.

○ Go to **Modify, Canvas, Image size**. Check the resolution is set to **72dpi** and click **OK**.

○ Next choose **Modify, Canvas, Canvas size**. Change **pixels** to **centimeters** and make the size **28 cm** wide and **18 cm** high. Click **OK**.

Figure 10.2: Changing the canvas size

The rabbit will probably not fit on the canvas. Don't panic! We will fix this shortly.

○ In the **Layers** panel, rename **Layer 1** as **BaseCampBunny**.

 ○ Let's hide the rabbit while we set up the grid. First, press the little – sign on the **BaseCampBunny** layer to collapse all the objects in the layer. Then press the **Show/Hide** icon (in the shape of an eye) to hide the rabbit.

Editing and displaying the grid

The grid needs to be switched on and edited so you can measure out the card with guides.

○ Click **Modify, Canvas, Canvas Size** and round the number of pixels so it can be divided by **20**. I made my card **800** wide and **500** high. Click **OK**.

○ Now select **View, Grid, Edit Grid**. Edit your grid so you have squares of **20 pixels**. If the grid is not displayed, click **View, Grid, Show Grid**.

○ Make sure the rulers and guides are displayed and mark out your card with guides (see Figure 10.3).

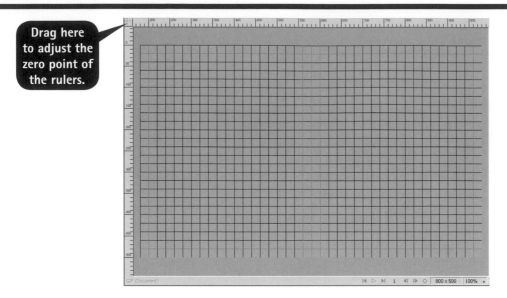

Figure 10.3: Marked-out card

Tip: You can drag the cross-hairs at the intersection of the ruler lines to line up the zero position of the horizontal and vertical rulers with the top left corner of the card.

Scaling the vector drawing

○ Switch the **Base Camp Bunny** layer back on.

○ **Zoom out** so you can see the entire bunny.

○ With the **Pointer** tool, drag a selection right across the bunny.

 ○ Pick the **Scale** tool in the **Tools** panel and scale the bunny head down so it fits on the right-hand page, using the guides to make the head nice and central.

Tip: Press **Ctrl-Space** and **left click** to zoom in and **Ctrl-Alt-Space left click** to zoom out if you need to.

Figure 10.4: Positioning Base Camp Bunny

○ Save the card again as **RabbitCardV1** in **BirthdayCard\Artwork**.

Taking a screenshot

A great tip for recording the stages of your work is to use screen grabs. You can take screenshots of anything from Internet sites to a computer game, and edit or crop them in Fireworks. You'll take a screenshot of the canvas with its rulers and guides, and save it in **BirthdayCard\Development**.

 ● If you cannot see the whole canvas on the screen, click the **Zoom** tool, right click on your canvas and choose **Fit All** (or press **Ctrl-0**).

● Press the **Print Screen** key, usually found in the top right corner of your keyboard.

● From the **Menu** bar, select **File**, **New**, and press **OK** as Fireworks has already changed the canvas size ready for the screenshot.

● Right click and **Fit All** again.

● Press **Ctrl-V** to paste (or select **Edit**, **Paste**).

● You may need to turn off the grid and guides so that you can see your screenshot more clearly.

 ● You will have captured and pasted the entire screen, so choose the **Crop** tool and drag a crop box over the part you want to keep. You can edit the size of the box by moving the black nodes. Press **Enter** when you're finished.

● Save your screen grab as **RabbitAndGrid.png** in **BirthdayCard\Development**.

● You can close this file now and we will continue with the birthday card. If you turned off the grid and guides, turn them on again now.

Adding text

● Make a new layer and name it **Circle**. Drag the new layer underneath the **BaseCampBunny** layer.

 ● Draw a big red circle on the **Circle** layer using the vector **Ellipse** tool, keeping the **Shift** key pressed while you draw it.

 ● Use the **Text** tool to write **Happy Birthday** on this layer. You will attach it to the circular path in the next step.

● Draw another, smaller circle and position it over the first. Then click the **Pointer** tool and press **Shift** to select both the new circle and the text.

● From the **Menu** bar, select **Text**, **Attach to Path**.

● Double-click the **Text** tool and use the **Text Editor** to tweak the text. When you are satisfied with the first **Happy Birthday**, edit the text to add a second one running round the bottom of the circle.

● You may need to scale the bunny again to get the text to fit nicely around it.

Figure 10.5: Attach to Path

I added a **Radial blur** from the **Live filters** to give the text a bit of movement – be very careful that you can still read it.

Adding a text background

To finish off the front and back of the card, you can make a background composed entirely of text. You will start by positioning the text on the left-hand page.

○ Make a new layer, and call it **TextBackground**. Drag the new layer so that it is underneath the other two layers.

○ Write **BASE CAMP** three times in a fairly small (say, 16 point) grey font.

○ Use the **Pointer** tool to position the text inside the guides.

Figure 10.6: Positioning the text box

○ With the new text selected, double-click the **Text** tool icon in the **Tools** panel; use the **Stretched Alignment** button to stretch the text across the text box.

○ Click **OK**.

Next you need to select the text and copy and paste it so you get a block of text.

○ Make sure the background text is selected and double-click the **Text** tool.

○ The **BASE CAMP** text will be selected so press **Ctrl–C** to copy the text, click at the end of the text and press **Enter**. Press **Ctrl–V** to paste the text. Press **Enter** and **Ctrl–V** again and repeat until you have a page of text. Press **OK** to confirm the change.

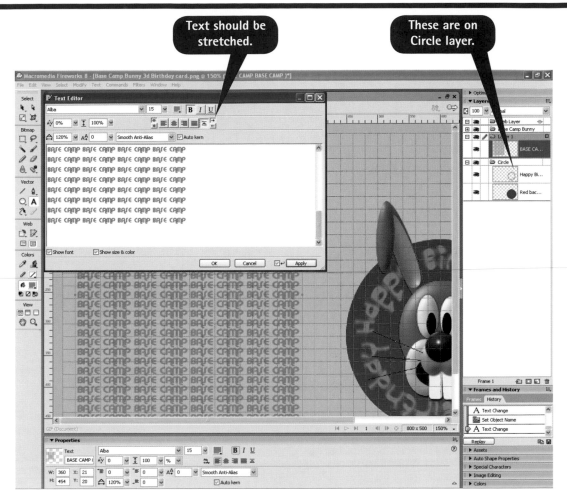

Figure 10.7: Repeat copy and paste

● In the **Layers** panel, click on the **Text** object in the **TextBackground** layer, and drag it onto the **New Bitmap Image** icon to clone the text.

● Use the **Pointer** tool to drag the text over to the right page, keeping the **Shift** key pressed to lock the text into a horizontal plane.

● Change the canvas colour to a colour of your choice by going to the **Menu** bar and selecting **Modify, Canvas, Canvas Color**.

Tip: How about using one of the 'corporate colours' from the logo?

This is a good moment to adjust colours and make tweaks to your card. You could add a logo to the back of the card.

Figure 10.8: Card with background

▶ This bit is up to you! If you want to put some text on the inside of your card, make a **New Layer**. Call it **InsideCardText**.

▶ Hide your other layers but keep the guides.

▶ Add a birthday greeting from the Base Camp staff and kids!

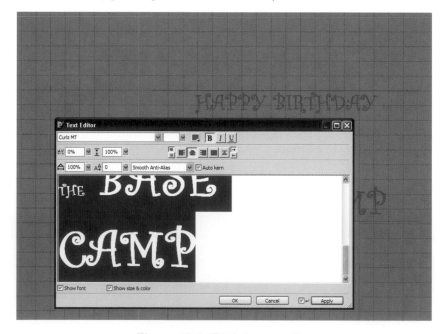

Figure 10.9: Birthday greeting

▶ Save the final version with a new name in **BirthdayCard\Artwork**.

Creating a Postcard

11

In this chapter you will look at how to put text onto two different photographs to make postcards that could be sold at Base Camp.

When graphic artists produce artwork for a project like this they have to think of ideas that will strengthen the brand – in this case Base Camp, an activity centre for 9–14 year-olds.

Branding can be achieved in many ways – for example by using a logo, a colour scheme, a font or a particular image. Think of McDonald's® – the logo is the Golden Arches® letter M, the colour scheme is red and yellow, the font is very distinctive and a key figure is Ronald McDonald® the clown.

You have already created a logo, which uses the colours blue, yellow and green. You have Base Camp Bunny as a kind of mascot. If this is used over and over, it will make people think of Base Camp whenever they see it. You have also used a particular typeface throughout. Any publicity material you produce should use the corporate colours, the corporate typeface and display the logo, the mascot or both.

The postcards will be sent to friends outside the camp and you can use them to advertise the camp by making it look like a fun place to be. Adding a logo and using the Base Camp colours and typeface will help to strengthen the brand and keep it in people's minds.

You can add messages to persuade people that Base Camp is a fantastic place to go and have fun – you must try to sell this idea with pictures, snappy tag lines and text.

Let's start the postcard.

● Open the picture **Abseiling.jpg**, which you should already have downloaded from **www.payne–gallway.co.uk** to your **DownloadedImages** folder. If you can't see it, set the **Files of type** box to **All readable files**.

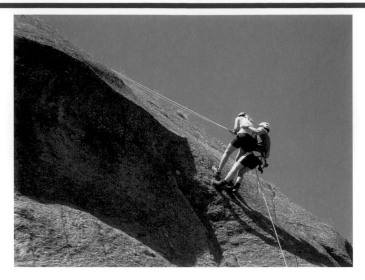

Figure 11.1: Abseiling ©Acorn Adventure

▷ Turn off the grid (if it is still on) by clicking **View**, **Grid** and deselecting **Show Grid**.

Painting the logo on the rocks

The first stage is to add the logo. To add a touch of originality, you can make it look as though it has been painted onto the rock face.

▷ Open your last version of the Base Camp logo.

▷ In the **Layers** panel, select each object by holding down **Ctrl** and left-clicking each object (on every layer) in turn. This will select all of your vector shapes.

▷ Go to **Modify**, **Group**. Your Base Camp logo is now ready to be moved in one grouped vector shape.

▷ Press **Ctrl-C** to copy the logo. Click the **Abseiling.jpg** tab at the top of your canvas.

▷ Make a new layer and call it **BaseCampLogo**.

▷ Press **Ctrl-V** to paste the logo into your new layer.

▷ With the Base Camp logo selected, go to **Modify, Transform, Distort**. Move the black nodes to make the logo look natural on the rocks – look at Figure 11.2 for reference.

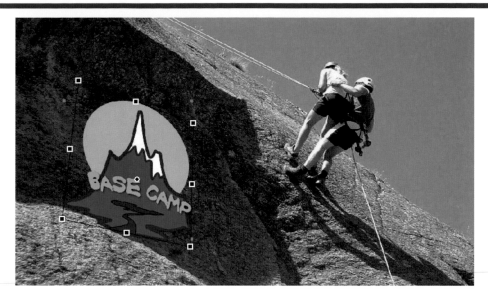

Figure 11.2: Distorting the logo

⊙ At the top of the **Layers** panel, change the **Blend mode** from **Normal** to **Overlay** to blend the logo into the rock (see Figure 11.3).

Colour sampling

⊙ Make a new layer and call it **Message**.

 ⊙ Use the vector **Rectangle** tool to draw a rectangle on the right-hand side.

We will fill the rectangle with a colour from the logo. We need to sample the colour to make sure it is identical. We can get the colour in several ways; here is one of them.

⊙ Change the **Blend mode** of the **Base Camp Logo** layer back to **Normal**.

⊙ Now select the rectangle either by using the **Pointer** tool or by clicking on its thumbnail in the **Layers** panel.

⊙ Click on the **Fill color box** in the **Properties inspector** and move the **Eyedropper** icon over to the logo, then click on the colour you want to sample. I chose a blue because I felt it made the sky look even bigger and didn't detract from the impact of the image.

Final touches

⊙ Next add some text. Think of something witty to say. Use the same or similar typeface and colours as your logo – this will help to tie your products together and give them a coherent look.

⊙ Redo the **Blend mode** of the logo.

⊙ Save your file as **AbseilingPostcard.png** in your **Exercises** folder. Close the file, but leave the **BaseCampLogo** file open.

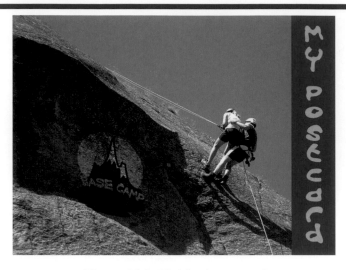

Figure 11.3: Finished postcard

Creating a feeling of movement

Some campers might prefer a postcard like the one shown in Figure 11.4; we can create an impression of high-octane action.

○ Open the image **RockJumping.jpg**.

You need to make a copy of the layer because the blur filter that we are going to apply sometimes makes the canvas edges transparent.

○ Drag the **Bitmap** thumbnail image onto the **New Bitmap Image** icon in the **Layers** panel.

○ Make sure the top **Bitmap** is selected, then apply a **live filter**: **Blur**, **Radial Blur**. Not too much – look at mine in Figure 11.4.

Figure 11.4: Radial blur ©Acorn Adventure

○ Save the file as **RockJump.png** in your **Exercises** folder.

Adding custom colours to the Swatches panel

We will add some text and graphics to this image, and we want them to use the same colours that are used in the logo. You can add all the colours from the logo to the **Swatches** panel, so that whatever graphic you are working on, they will always be handy.

● Click the **BaseCampLogo.png** tab, or open the file if it isn't already open.

● With the logo in front of you, open the **Colors** panel. You can do this by selecting **Window, Color Mixer** from the **Menu** bar.

● In the **Colors** panel, click the **Swatches** tab.

● Press **Ctrl-D** to make sure that nothing is selected.

● Add the first colour to the **Colors** panel by clicking the **Eyedropper** tool on a colour in the logo and then moving the mouse pointer into the grey area under the swatches. It turns into a **Paint Bucket** tool, so just click again.

● Add all your logo colours!

● Click the **Options** box at the top right of the **Colors** panel. Select **Save Swatches** and save your swatch as **LogoSwatch** in your **Components** folder.

Figure 11.5: Swatches panel

Adding text and a dotted line

● Return to your **RockJump** postcard.

● Make a new layer and call it **TextLayer**.

● Using the **Text** tool, type **Rock Jump**. Use the **Colors** panel to pick the light blue colour from the logo.

● Click **Modify, Transform, Distort**. Try to match the text to Figure 11.6. I am trying to make the text look as though it is lying on the water.

Figure 11.6: Text on water

Tip: By doing lots of sketching, you will develop a good understanding of how perspective works – extremely useful in the world of graphics. Remember that as objects get further away, they appear smaller. Try to look at the direction in which shadows are cast and how reflections work on different surfaces.

 ◐ Click the **Pen** tool and set the **Tip size** to **10**, the **Stroke category** to **Dashed, Heavy Dash**. Use a colour from the logo.

◐ Draw an arc from the launch point to the splash-down point. Double-click the last point to finish the line.

Figure 11.7: Jump line

◐ You can add an arrowhead to the line by going to **Commands, Creative, Add Arrowheads**.

Figure 11.8: Adding arrowheads

Tip: The line and the arrowhead will be grouped together, so use the **Subselection** tool if you decide to change their colours.

○ Add three more text objects: **Jump**, **Free Fall** and **Impact Zone**. Use a colour from the **LogoSwatch** and make sure they are three separate pieces of text, as we will need to move them independently.

Figure 11.9: Journey to the Impact Zone

○ Copy and paste the logo into the top left corner of your postcard.

○ Play with the **Layer Blend modes** and colours. I added a splash made with the **Pen** tool – my effort is in Figure 11.10.

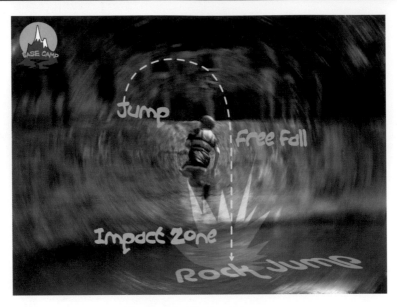

Figure 11.10: Rock jumper

▶ Save your card as **RockJumpV2** in your **Exercises** folder.

Masks and Montage

Masks can be created to cover existing objects and determine the area of the image that is visible. We'll start by doing a practice exercise to understand exactly how they work.

▶ Create a new canvas with a **Width** of **1200 Pixels**, a **Height** of **850 Pixels**, a **Resolution** of **72 Pixels/Inch** and the **Canvas color** set to **Transparent**.

▶ Press **Ctrl-0** (**Ctrl** and **zero**), the shortcut to **Fit All**. (Alternatively, use the **Zoom** tool, right-click on the canvas and select **Fit All**.)

▶ Go to **File**, **Import (Ctrl-R)**. Choose **Archery.jpg** from **DownloadedImages** and click **Open**.

▶ Drag the right-angle icon to fit easily in the canvas and then release it.

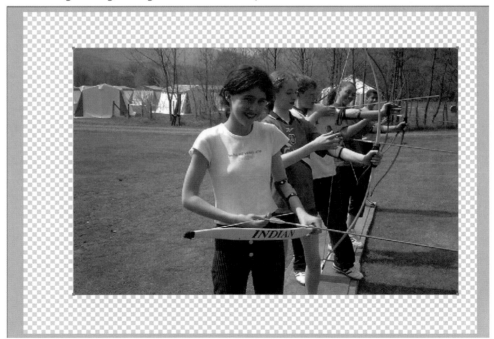

Figure 12.1: ©Acorn Adventure

The first mask we will create will be a vector ellipse.

Use the vector **Ellipse** tool to draw an ellipse over the centre of the picture. You can use any **Fill** colour and you don't need a Stroke (see Figure 12.2).

Figure 12.2: Creating a mask object

▶ With the mask selected, choose **Edit**, **Cut** from the **Menu** bar.

▶ Select the original image and, from the **Menu** bar, choose **Edit**, **Paste as Mask**.

Only the part of the image that is inside the mask is now visible.

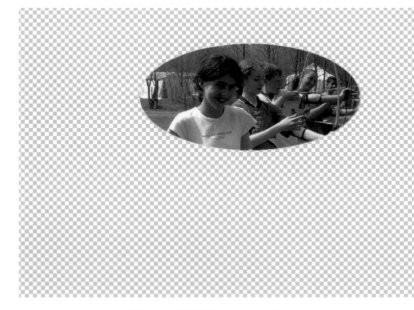

Figure 12.3: The masked image

▶ Look in the **Layers** panel (see Figure 12.4). The bitmap object shows both the image and the mask. The two objects are linked, shown by a little chain between them.

Figure 12.4: Linked objects

Try moving the masked image using the **Pointer** tool. The image and mask move together.

You can, however, unlink the image from the mask and move it separately. Click the link between the image and mask in the **Layers** panel so that it disappears. Now try moving the mask. You can mask a different part of the picture.

Figure 12.5: Moving the mask separately from the image

Notice that the mask, not the image, is currently selected in the **Layers** panel. You can select the image and move or size it.

Click between the image and the mask to relink the two objects. Now you can move them together.

When you have finished experimenting, drag the object (image and mask) to the trashcan to delete it.

A bitmap mask

Now you will try a bitmap mask, which you will create using the **Brush** tool. This is the technique you will use for the montage.

◉ Import the **Archery.jpg** file again, and make it a similar size to what it was before.

 ◉ Select the **Bitmap** object by clicking its thumbnail in the **Layers** panel, and click the **Add Mask** icon.

◉ In the **Layers** panel, a **Mask** symbol appears in the object box.

◉ Click the **Brush** tool in the **Tools** panel. Choose a brush size of **80** with **Basic**, **Soft Rounded** stroke category and **100%** opacity.

You can use a useful shortcut to make your masking easier.

◉ Make sure you are working on a mask layer, and in your **Tools** panel find the **Colors** section.

◉ Make the **Stroke color** box **white** and the **Fill color** box **black**.

Figure 12.6: Setting the mask colour

◉ Press **X** on the keyboard and you will notice they swap position.

◉ Paint with your mask and press **X** to reverse what you have done.

Figure 12.7: A softer mask

Note: If the image is selected instead of the mask in the **Layers** panel, you will paint a mess over the image!

◑   Delete this layer without saving. We're ready for the real thing!

Making a montage

In this exercise we will make a montage of images – it will be up to you where you place them but I will add lots of explanations as we go.

We will use layer masks to make the images merge together. You will need to use your artistic skills to blend each image, using natural boundaries such as an arm or a rock to make breaks or borders between images. Get good at this and you will be on your way to a career in the graphics world.

Using secondary sources

For the montage, we will use nine photographs originally downloaded from the website **www.acornadventure.co.uk** and saved on the Payne-Gallway website.

Tip: Remember to enter all secondary images in your **Elements** table (see page 7).

Note: Acknowledge the sources and get permission to use them if necessary. (Permission has already been kindly given by the managing director of Acorn Adventure to use these photographs for this purpose.)

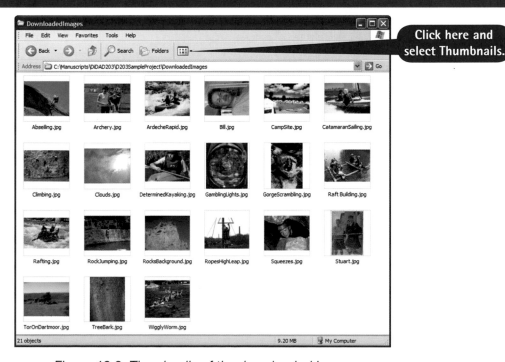

Figure 12.8: Thumbnails of the downloaded images

Importing images for the montage

▶ Create a new canvas with a **Width** of **1200 Pixels**, a **Height** of **850 Pixels**, a **Resolution** of **72 Pixels/Inch** and the **Canvas color** set to **Transparent**.

▶ Press **Ctrl-0** (**Ctrl** and **zero**), the shortcut to **Fit All**. (Alternatively, use the **Zoom** tool – right click on the canvas and select **Fit All**.)

▶ Go to **File, Import (Ctrl-R)**. Choose **RaftBuilding.jpg** from **DownloadedImages** and click **Open**.

▶ Drag the right-angle icon to the approximate size you want and release. Position and size the image to match Figure 12.9. To resize without distorting an image, hold down the **Shift** key while you drag a corner handle.

Figure 12.9: Importing an image

▶ Import all the pictures in the order below, sizing and positioning them roughly as in Figure 12.10. You need to make sure all the images are overlapping each other by quite a bit, so that you can blend one image into the other without the transparent background showing through.

1.   (**RaftBuilding.jpg** – done already)

2.   **Climbing.jpg**

3.   **WigglyWorm.jpg**

4.   **GorgeScrambling.jpg**

5.   **Archery.jpg**

6.   **Squeezes.jpg**

7.   **ArdecheRapid.jpg**

8.   **Rafting.jpg**

9.   **DeterminedKayaking.jpg**

▶ Rename the layer objects (currently all called **Bitmap**) using these file names.

Figure 12.10: Montage before blending

Blending the images using masks

Let's start with **Squeezes**.

Select the **Squeezes** layer by clicking its name in the **Layers** panel, then click the **Add Mask** icon.

In the **Layers** panel, a **Mask** symbol appears in the **Squeezes** object box.

Figure 12.11: The mask symbol

Remember that you can select either the mask or the image in the object box. If you want to move or paint the image, select the image. If you want to move or paint the mask, select the mask.

◓   Click the **Brush** tool in the **Tools** panel. Choose a large **Basic**, **Soft Rounded** brush with about **50%** opacity. (Using a 50% opacity will allow you to blend the different images more easily.)

Use the shortcut (explained again below) to make creating your montage easier and faster.

◓   Make sure you are working on a mask object. In your **Tools** panel make the **Stroke color** box **black** and the **Fill color** box **white**.

◓   Paint with your **Brush** tool and press **X** if you want to reverse what you have done. You can use this procedure on all your masks, so remember to set the **Stroke** and **Fill** colours as the first thing you do each time.

◓   Paint out the rocks to show the archer, as shown in Figure 12.12.

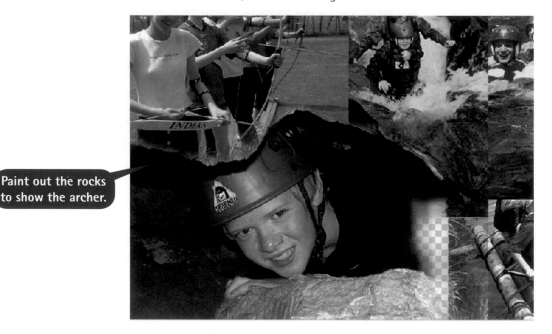

Figure 12.12: Blending the images

◓   Click on the **Archery** layer, then click the **Add Mask** icon.

◓   From the **Tools** panel, choose the **Paintbrush** tool, **Stroke** colour **black** and **Fill** colour **white**. Merge the **Archery** layer into the **Gorge Scramble**.

◓   Continue in a clockwise direction, adding masks and carefully blending the images into each other. Use the pointer tool to find out which image may need to be masked.

Figure 12.13: Take care!

Tip: Don't forget that you can use **Ctrl**, **Space bar** and **left click** to zoom in. Press the **Alt** button as well to zoom out, and keep the **Space bar** pressed while you scroll around the canvas.

Here is my montage.

Figure 12.14: Montage

Save your montage as **BaseCampMontage.png** in your **Exercises** folder.

Cut-outs

In this chapter you will learn how to make neat **cut-outs**. This generally involves taking a photo of a product and very neatly cutting it out and placing it on a different background.

Tracing round the image

We will cut out a picture of someone jumping on an aerial tramway and give her a new background to make a much more punchy image.

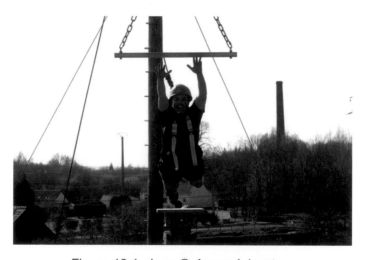

Figure 13.1: Jump© Acorn Adventure

○   Open picture **RopesHighLeap.jpg** from your **DownloadedImages** folder.

○   Click the **Pen** tool; you are going to draw a vector path around the jumping figure.

○   Make sure the **Properties inspector** shows the **Fill** set to **None** and the **Stroke** set to **1 pixel** and **Pencil, 1-Pixel Hard** (see Figure 13.2).

Figure 13.2: Pen tool properties

Before starting to draw the path, you need to zoom in so that you can see individual pixels.

This will help you to get the most accurate path around the jumper.

◐   By pressing **Ctrl** and the **Space bar** you can click to **zoom in** while the **Pen** tool is selected. (If you add the **Alt** key as well you will **zoom out**.)

◐   Pressing the **Space bar** on its own gives you the **Hand** tool, which you can use to click and drag the canvas in any direction.

◐   Draw a path all the way round the jumper as accurately as possible.

Figure 13.3: Carefully draw around the edge

Tip: Use the **Subselection** tool to tweak the path. Add extra nodes to your path by clicking the **Pen** tool on the path. Drawing the path is the most accurate way of cutting out; you could use the **Lasso** tool, but it is very difficult to get good results.

Figure 13.4: The completed path

Creating the bitmap mask

▶ With the path selected, change its **Fill** colour to match its **Stroke** colour.

▶ From the **Menu** bar select **Modify, Flatten Selection** to convert the vector path to a bitmap image. You will then be able to make a bitmap mask which you can edit with the **Brush** tool.

▶ From the **Menu** bar select **Edit, Cut**.

▶ Select the background bitmap image.

▶ From the **Menu** bar select **Edit, Paste as Mask**.

Your image should look like Figure 13.5. Save it as **HighLeap.png** in your **Exercises** folder.

Figure 13.5: Cut-out

Taking your own photos

It looks good, but you now need a background. You can find one in several ways; one of the best ways is to go outside with a digital camera and shoot a piece of sky (be careful not to look directly at the sun!). Each digital camera has its own way of working, so you'll have to read the instructions that come with your particular camera.

Which resolution setting?

Some cameras have a choice of image resolutions. Images that you take with a digital camera for printing out on photographic paper are best taken at the highest resolution your camera allows.

However, on-screen images are viewed at a resolution of 72 pixels per inch (or **dpi**, dots per inch). This means that you can get away with using a lower quality setting. It is always worth using the lowest setting you need. This prevents wasting space in your camera's memory, and also reduces the amount of optimisation you may need to do on the photo later on.

○ A 1 megapixel (or even 640 × 480 VGA) setting will be fine if you don't plan to enlarge a photo.

○ If you are taking a photo that you might want to enlarge significantly, you should use a higher resolution setting (3M or 5M).

These photos will still have relatively large file sizes and will be of a higher quality than needed for web purposes. You will learn to optimize photos and images later.

Viewing your photos in Microsoft® Windows Explorer

After you have downloaded your photos onto a computer, you will need to view them to select which ones you want to use. The easiest way to do this is to use Microsoft® Windows Explorer.

○ Open Windows Explorer and locate your **DownloadedImages** folder.

 ○ At the top of the window, click the **Views** icon in the **Shortcuts** bar. Select **Filmstrip** from the menu that appears. Use this to flick through your photos and decide which ones to use.

Figure 13.6: Viewing pictures

Tip: If there is no **Filmstrip** option shown, this may be because you have some movie files in that folder, so move them to another folder. If you still have no **Filmstrip** option, just double-click each photo to see a larger version of it. If you are using a different version of **Windows®**, click the **Thumbnails** option.

When you come to download your own photos from the camera to a PC, you should give sensible names to any that you think you will use so that you can find them again later easily.

Delete any that you won't use, so you don't end up with far too many photos!

Finding a ready-made background photo

Sometimes you will have to use an image from a library of photographs. When picking an image, you will need to be very critical about the quality of the photo. There is a lot you can do to fix colours and some damage, but if the photo suffers from a very poor resolution or 'noise' – a common problem of digital photography, caused by too little light – it would be better to carry on looking or to re-shoot it yourself.

Figure 13.7: Backgrounds

There are a number of websites that have free images. Try **http://www.freeimages.co.uk/**.

Loading a background

You will use an image from your **DownloadedImages** folder as a background for the cut-out.

> **Tip**: If you want to use your own background image, check that it is only around 1000 pixels wide – you don't need the image any bigger. If your image is too large, go to **Modify**, **Canvas**, **Image Size** and change it to 1000 pixels wide. To see the whole image on the canvas, click the **Zoom** tool, right-click on the canvas and select **Fit All**.

 ▶   Load **Clouds.jpg**.

 ▶   Click the **HighLeap.png** tab at the top of the canvas window.

 ▶   Select the thumbnail image of the jumper and press **Ctrl-C** to copy the **Background** layer with its mask attached.

 ▶   Click back to the **Clouds** image and press **Ctrl-V** to paste in the jumper.

Fixing problems

First, notice that the sun is on the wrong side of the jumper.

○ To fix this, select the **Jumper** layer and from the **Menu** bar select **Modify, Transform, Flip Horizontal**.

○ In the **Properties inspector**, add a **live filter**. Select **Adjust Colour, Brightness/Contrast** and change the settings to make the jumper look a bit punchier.

You may notice that the cut-out is not perfect. You can make adjustments to the mask as follows.

○ Click on the mask in the **Layers** panel; a selection box will appear around it, as shown in Figure 13.8.

Figure 13.8: Mask

○ Choose a small brush and load it with black. The **Properties inspector** should look like the one below.

Figure 13.9: Mask brush options

Remember that if you paint **black**, you will add more masking paint and you will mask the image to show what is behind it. If you paint **white**, you will remove part of the mask.

○ Try it first. Paint black over the image and notice how you can see through it now. Press **Ctrl-Z** to undo what you have done.

○ Now go around the edges and carefully clean up any problems. I had to use a 2 pixel brush around the fingers.

Tip: You might prefer to use the **Pencil** tool for this; you can use it to edit the individual pixels.

○ As a final touch, I used a **live filter** on the cloud background. Select **Adjust Colour, Hue/Saturation**. Check the **Colorize** box and use the sliders to make a perfect sky blue.

All done!

Figure 13.10: Free as a bird!

▶ Save your picture as **HighLeapSky.png** in your **Exercises** folder.

Using Pre-prepared Images

14

You are going to use the montage we created in Chapter 12 and some other images you have completed to produce a brochure front and back cover.

Combining objects into one layer

▶   Open **BaseCampMontage.png**.

You need to combine all the objects into a single object (called **flattening**) because the result will be much easier to use.

▶   Select **Layer 1** in the **Layers** panel. This automatically selects all the objects within it.

▶   Go to **Modify, Flatten Selection**. You are left with a single object in the layer.

▶   You will need to change the canvas size because the **.png** format retains information – such as the fact that the images bleed off the edge of the canvas.

▶   Go to **Modify, Canvas, Canvas Size**. It should read **1200** pixels by **850**. Click **OK**.

You will notice the blue selection line jump back to the canvas edges.

▶   Save the file as **BaseCampMontageFlat.png** in your **Exercises** folder.

▶   Close this file.

Making a brochure cover

In this exercise you will use the montage, with effects added, as a background for a brochure cover.

▶   Open your saved **BrochureInside.png**, which should be in your **Exercises** folder.

▶   Select and delete the text and resave this file into the same folder, giving it the new file name **BrochureFrontAndBackCover.png**.

▶   Check that the grid is visible (**View, Grid, Show Grid**) and the guides are all in position.

▶   Go to **View, Guides, Edit Guides**, and change the guides to a bright red – if they aren't already.

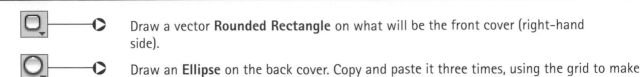

Draw a vector **Rounded Rectangle** on what will be the front cover (right-hand side).

Draw an **Ellipse** on the back cover. Copy and paste it three times, using the grid to make the cover look like the one in Figure 14.1.

Tip: You can easily get the top and bottom ellipses in the right position by snapping them to the grid. You can then select all four ellipses and use **Modify**, **Align**, **Distribute Heights** to set the vertical positions of the middle two ellipses.

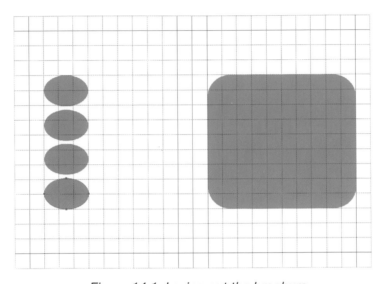

Figure 14.1: Laying out the brochure

You can combine the shapes with a rectangle covering the whole canvas so that the green shapes will become holes through which images will be visible.

Draw a vector **Rectangle** from top right to bottom left – it must cover the entire canvas.

Select all the objects by clicking on the layer name, **Layer 1**.

Go to **Modify**, **Combine Paths**, **Join**.

Now change the **Fill** colour in the **Properties inspector** to the dark blue colour from the logo. Remember that you can load your custom colours by clicking **Window**, **Swatches** on the **Menu** bar.

Use a **live filter (effect) Shadow and Glow** to add a **Drop Shadow**, which must go from left to right.

Figure 14.2: Drop Shadow options

▶ Drag the **Composite Path** object in the **Layers** panel down to the **New Bitmap Image** icon to duplicate the layer.

▶ Call the original composite path **Shape1** and the duplicated one above it **Shape2**.

Figure 14.3: Next stage

Adding an image as a vector mask

This bit is really cool!

▶ Select **File**, **Import** and choose the **BaseCampMontageFlat.png**.

▶ Draw the imported bitmap right across the canvas.

▶ Go to **Edit**, **Cut**.

▶ Select the layer **Shape2** and go to **Edit**, **Paste Inside**.

Now experiment with using this image in a more arty way by changing the canvas colour to a colour from the Base Camp logo.

▶ Select **Modify**, **Canvas**, **Canvas Color** and click the **Custom Color** box.

▶ Select the dark blue from the logo and click **OK**.

▶ Select the **Shape2** layer with the **Pointer** tool, and in the **Layers** panel change the **Blend modes** until you find one you like.

Figure 14.4: The blended brochure

Adding pre-prepared graphics

- ▶   Open the Base Camp logo, **BaseCampLogo.png**.

- ▶   Select all its objects and go to **Modify, Group**. This will group all the elements of the logo together, so it will be much easier to move.

- ▶   Click **Edit, Copy** and click back to **BrochureFrontAndBackCover.png**.

- ▶   Make a new layer and click **Edit, Paste**. You may get a message asking if you want to resample the image. Click **Don't resample**.

 ▶   Use the **Scale** tool to position the logo in the right-hand page recess.

- ▶   Drag down the layer containing the logo, so that it is the last layer in the **Layers** panel.

For the following steps you will need the files **CatamaranSailing.png** and **Abseiling.png** from your **DownloadedImages** folder, and **HighLeapSky.png** and **WoodSign.png** from your **Exercises** folder.

- ▶   Open them, and if they are layered bitmap **.png** files, flatten them.

- ▶   Copy and paste them into **BrochureFrontAndBackCover.png**.

- ▶   Use the **Scale** tool to make them small enough to fit into the small ellipses when they are positioned. Use **Add mask** to crop them if they need it.

- ▶   Create a new top layer and add some suitable text.

If you want to, you could make the sun in the logo three-dimensional by selecting it with the **Subselection** tool and choosing a bevel from the **live filters** (**effects**) in the **Properties inspector**.

I even found room for the Base Camp Bunny! He's becoming a familiar face and an old friend, and that's just what we are trying to achieve to strengthen the brand.

◐   Save the cover in your **Exercises** folder.

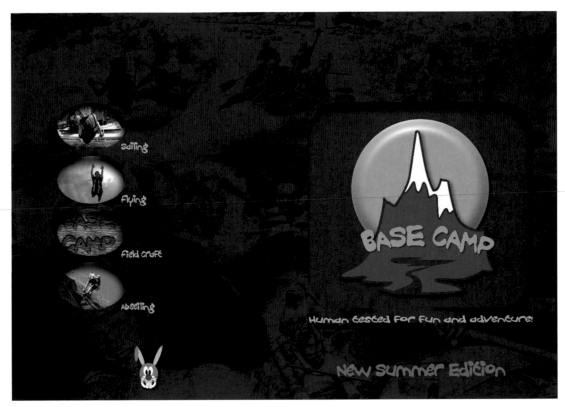

Figure 14.5: Finished brochure cover

◐   Close all of your files.

Fixing Problems with Photos

This chapter will cover some elements you have already learnt, but I hope you will see that it is much more in the context of how you could use Fireworks at home, college or the office. With that in mind, you could use digital photos or pictures you may have scanned to complete these projects. Alternatively, you can use photos downloaded from the Payne-Gallway website.

As well as fixing problems with photos, we'll look at capturing screenshots and improving scanned images.

First of all, we are going to look at ways of touching up a photograph that you might, for example, want to post on a website or email to a friend. Then we will 'repair' an old and scratched photo. Finally, we will look at how to sharpen blurred images.

Removing red-eye

Red-eye is a common problem in photography, happening when the camera flash reflects from the eye. You can use Fireworks to remove this unsightly effect. You either need a picture of a friend with a bad case of red-eye, or you can download the image **Bill.jpg** from **www.payne-gallway.co.uk**.

○ Open your photo in Fireworks.

If you are using **Bill.jpg**, you first need to rotate the image.

○ From the **Menu** bar, select **Modify, Canvas, Rotate 90 CW**.

Figure 15.1: Photo of Bill with red-eye

Tip: If you use **Modify**, **Transform**, **Rotate 90 CW**, it will rotate the layer but not the canvas, leaving you with a canvas that does not match the image size.

◐ Zoom in on one of Bill's eyes so that you can get the most accurate possible selection.

 ◐ Select the **Oval Marquee** tool and, in the **Properties inspector**, set the **Style** to **Normal** and the **Edge** to **Feather**, **2**. You want to soften the selected edge to make your changes undetectable.

◐ Draw a selection over Bill's eye, covering the whole of the coloured iris.

◐ With the **Shift** key held down, draw another selection over the other eye. You can press **Ctrl-Z** to undo it if you don't place it perfectly the first time.

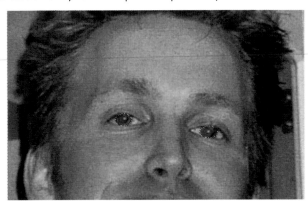

Figure 15.2: Selecting the red eyes

◐ In the **Menu** bar, go to **Filters**, **Adjust Color**, **Hue/Saturation**. Adjust the settings: you will need to reduce the **Saturation** and move the **Hue** to your chosen eye colour. Don't change the **Lightness**, as it will muddy the image. Click **OK** when you're finished.

◐ This time go to **Filters**, **Adjust Colour**, **Brightness/Contrast**. By tweaking the contrast you can eliminate unwanted reflections or highlights. Have a play and find the setting that looks most realistic.

Figure 15.3: Fixed

▶ For some fun, we will add a picture frame. From the **Menu** bar, select **Commands**, **Creative**, **Add Picture Frame**.

Figure 15.4: Add Picture Frame

▶ Choose a **pattern** and type in a **Frame Size** and press **OK**. You can undo and choose different options to explore what Fireworks has to offer.

Note: The frame is automatically added as a new object, so you have the option to switch it on and off.

Figure 15.5: Padlock

▶ Add a drop shadow to the frame. You will need to go to the **Layers** panel and click the **Padlock** to unlock the layer.

Figure 15.6: All done

▶ Save the image as **FixedRedEye.png** in your **Exercises** folder.

Scratched and dusty old photos

You will need to scan an old and damaged photo, or you can download the image below from **www.payne-gallway.co.uk**.

Figure 15.7: Old photo in need of fixing

● Open the picture called **Stuart.jpg**.

● The image is quite faded, so go to **Filters, Adjust Color, Auto Levels**.

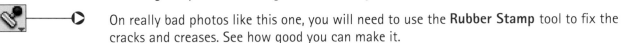 ● On really bad photos like this one, you will need to use the **Rubber Stamp** tool to fix the cracks and creases. See how good you can make it.

● Lastly, choose the **Marquee** tool to draw a square just inside the white frame of the photo. Go to **Select**, **Select Inverse** and paint the selection white. That will help clean up the photo.

Figure 15.8: Finished job

◐ Produce a **Before and After** image to show how good your re-touching skills are!

◐ Save the final result in your **Exercises** folder and close the file.

Sharpening blurred images

Quite often, images are blurred. There is a filter that can help to solve this problem. However, although images that are blurred can be made usable, they will never be as good as a sharp original!

Let's load a blurred image and experiment with some **Sharpening** effects.

◐ Open **GamblingLights.jpg**.

Figure 15.9: Blurred image

There are two preset sharpening filters: **Sharpen** and **Sharpen More**. These are designed to tighten up most images.

◐ Go to **Filters**, **Sharpen**, **Sharpen**.

◐ Now undo and redo (using **Ctrl-Z** and **Ctrl-Y**) to observe how much the **Sharpen** filter affected the image.

◐ Undo the **Sharpen** effect and try the **Sharpen More** filter. Undo it again.

◐ Now try the **Unsharp Mask** – despite its name, this does actually sharpen the image. I always use the **Unsharp Mask** as it gives me more control.

Figure 15.10: Unsharp Mask panel

◉ Produce **Before** and **After** images to show how well it works.

Figure 15.11: Fixed

Note that if you sharpen the image too much you will get a white haloing effect and the image will break up into blocks of colour.

Figure 15.12: The haloing effect

Print Screen

This is a very useful function to capture an image of what is on your screen. You might use it if you are surfing the web and you find some information you need, or if you need a screen grab to show how you created a particular graphic. You can try it out now.

It doesn't matter if you have Fireworks running or not.

◉ Press the **Print Screen** key at the top of your keyboard. This will copy a snapshot of your screen to the **Clipboard**.

◉ Open Fireworks (if it is not already open).

◉ Select **File**, **New**.

The **Canvas Size** and **Image Size** will be set already, depending on the size and resolution of your screen.

Figure 15.13: Preset canvas size

◉ Click **OK**.

◉ Click **Edit**, **Paste (Ctrl-V)**, and the screen grab will appear. You can crop or change it like any raster image.

An alternative to using **Print Screen** is to use a screen capture utility program – there are many free ones available that are good.

Tip: You can use **Alt-Print Screen** to just grab the current window.

Fixing problems with scanned images

We covered the basics of scanning in Chapter 7. When you scan a page, remember that you could be infringing copyright if you use it without permission.

Before you start scanning, work out how large you want the image to be in the web page or printed page you are about to produce. Then make sure you use a suitable resolution for either screen or print.

Sometimes you may get a **moiré** effect, as in Figure 15.14, which makes the scan appear patterned or stripey. Here are a few ideas to get around this problem. Trying to fix images is not an exact science – in most cases you can only improve an image – and getting a perfect result is rare.

Figure 15.14: Moiré effect

You can see the **moiré** pattern appear, and it will look much worse in print than it looks on screen.

You can get rid of it, or at least make it better, by scanning the image at full resolution.

◐   You could try scanning the cover of this book or a magazine!

◐   When your image is scanned into Fireworks, go to **Filters**, **Noise**, **Add noise**. This will help to break up the **moiré** print screen; you will need less than **10** as the **Amount**.

◐   Then use **Modify**, **Canvas**, **Image size** to resize your scan depending on how you plan to use it. It will pay to repeat the process with varying amounts of noise. Even slightly changing the scan resolution may help.

Printed Artwork   **16**

The Base Camp dollar

In this chapter we will look at producing artwork for print. The Base Camp dollar note will be used instead of money within the camp, so it obviously has to be printed. Artwork for high quality printed material (such as this book) requires a resolution of **300dpi** to ensure that images are smooth and not pixellated.

Images using such a high resolution will result in files much larger than anything you have produced so far. A large layered computer file can run into many hundreds of megabytes!

For this exercise, though, we will use a resolution of **72dpi** for the design of the dollar note. We will also only show one side.

It will help your design if you find some images of paper money ... you might even have some in your pocket. Measure different notes and decide on a good size for the new dollar note. Have a look at what is printed on the front and back of a note and the type of background used.

◗   Make a list of elements you need to include.

◗   Create a new canvas with a **Width** of **14 cm**, a **Height** of **7.5 cm**, a **Resolution** of **72 Pixels/Inch** and the **Canvas color** set to **White**.

Figure 16.1: Settings for the Base Camp dollar

Creating the background

First of all, you will create the intricate background found on money as a deterrent to forgery.

○ Press **Ctrl-0** to fit your canvas onto the screen.

○ Choose the **Pen** tool and change the **Stroke** to **black**, the **Size** to **2**, the **Stroke category** to **Pencil**, **1-Pixel Hard** and the **Edge** to **0** so you get a hard-edged line.

○ Draw a single wavy line across the canvas, starting and ending the line slightly off your canvas, as shown in Figure 16.2.

Figure 16.2: Wavy line

○ Click the **Pointer** tool and select the line. As you start to move it down press the **Shift** key and the **Alt** key, which will drag-copy the line and keep it in the same vertical plane.

○ Go to **Edit**, **Repeat Duplicate** (**Ctrl-Y**) and keep duplicating until you cover the canvas.

○ Keep going into the grey at the bottom of the canvas – you will move the wavy lines up in the next step, and need them to completely cover the canvas when you do.

Figure 16.3: Multiple wavy lines

○ Click **Layer 1** in the **Layers** panel to select all your lines and use the **Pointer** tool to drag all the lines up to cover the canvas.

> You may need to drag-copy some more lines to fill these gaps.

Figure 16.4: Selecting and dragging

You don't need to tweak these vector lines and they are already print size, so you can turn these into a bitmap layer for the next stage.

○ Click the name **Layer 1** again. This time, when all the lines are selected, go to **Modify**, **Flatten Selection**.

○ Change the name of this bitmap object from **Bitmap** to **Lines** and drag it down onto the **New Bitmap Image** icon to make a duplicate of it.

○ Flip this image using **Modify**, **Transform**, **Flip Horizontal**.

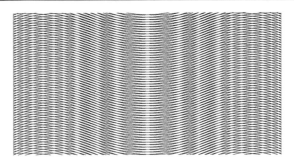

Figure 16.5: Criss-crossed wavy lines

○ Rename this layer **CrissCrossLines**.

○ Make a **New Layer** called **GradientBackground** and drag it under **CrissCrossLines**.

○ Drag the vector **Rectangle** tool right over the canvas. Turn off the **Stroke**, choose a **Fill** colour to look like the washy sort of colours used for paper money and add a **Fill Texture**. I chose **Hatch 3** at **50%**.

Figure 16.6: Fill properties for the background

○ Draw another vector rectangle over the canvas, and this time in the **Properties inspector** select a **Fill category** of **Gradient**, **Bars**.

○ Click in the **Fill Color** box and choose **Cobalt Blue** from the **Preset**.

○ At the top of the **Layers** panel, set the **Layer Blend mode** to **Fuzzy Light**. (If you haven't got this layer blend, set the **Opacity** to **40%** instead.)

○ Go back to your **CrissCrossLines** layer, and set the **Opacity** to **30**.

○ Use the **Crop** tool to trim your wavy lines to the canvas size.

Figure 16.7: The completed background

○ Save the image as **BaseCampDollar.png** in your **Dollar** folder.

Adding a photograph and mask

You will add a picture for the note; you can use a picture that you have taken yourself or use the one I used.

▶ Open the picture **TorOnDartmoor.jpg**. You should already have downloaded this from **www.payne-gallway.co.uk** into your **DownloadedImages** folder.

▶ Select it and copy it using either **Edit**, **Copy** or **Ctrl-C**.

▶ Click back onto the tab for **BaseCampDollar.png**.

▶ Make a new layer called **Photograph** and paste the picture onto it. You might get a panel asking if you want to resample the image – if so, select **Don't Resample**.

Figure 16.8: Resample or not?

 ▶ Use the **Scale** tool to size and position the image. Draw an **Oval Marquee** tool over the most interesting bit of the picture.

 ▶ Press the **Add Mask** icon.

Figure 16.9: Picture cut-out

You will use the **Find edges** filter to make the photo look a bit like an engraving, just like real paper money.

 ▶ Duplicate the oval photo by dragging the **Bitmap** object onto the **New Bitmap** icon.

▶ In the **Menu** bar select **Filters**, **Other**, **Find Edges**.

○ The image will be mostly black; let's reverse it so the black becomes white. Go to **Filters**, **Adjust Colour**, **Invert**.

○ Check the order of the layers in the **Layers** panel. You should have **GradientBackground** at the bottom, then **CrissCrossLines**, and **Photograph** at the top.

○ In **Photograph**, select the image we applied the **Find Edges** filter to. Set the **Opacity** to **66** and the **Blend mode** to **Luminosity**. You can do this either in the **Properties inspector** (if you have the **Pointer** tool selected) or in the **Layers** panel.

○ Set the unfiltered photo image (underneath the other one in the **Photograph** layer) to **100% Opacity** and set its **Blend mode** to **Screen**.

○ Draw a vector **Ellipse** around the photo image, drag it under your photo images and set its **Blend mode** to **Luminosity**.

 ○ Use the **Scale** tool to tweak it around your photo image so that it looks something like Figure 16.10.

Figure 16.10: Adding an ellipse

Adding text

It doesn't look much like real money at the moment, so let's add some text. This will be largely up to you – I used frilly **Edwardian** text to give it an authentic look.

○ Add a new layer called **Text**. Keep in mind what real money looks like and start adding text to make it look as authentic as possible. Figure 16.11 shows what I did.

Figure 16.11: Loot!

▶ Add a serial number! Use the **Scale** tool to spin the text around.

Using the Assets panel

There is one more thing you can do to add realism to your currency.

▶ Make a new layer called **VectorSymbol**, and make sure it is at the top.

▶ Open the **Assets** panel in your **Panel** dock. If you can't find it, go to **Window**, **Auto Shapes**.

▶ In the **Assets** panel there are some extra useful shapes. Click on **Perspective** and drag it onto your canvas. The perspective lines add a little extra interest.

▶ In the **Layers** panel, change the **Layer Blend mode** to **Overlay** or **Screen**.

▶ Tweak the layers to see if you can make your Base Camp dollar even better!

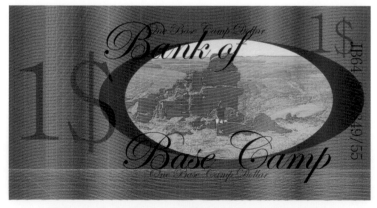

Figure 16.12: The completed Base Camp dollar

▶ Save your **BaseCampDollar.png** file in your **Dollar** folder.

Tip: Don't forget to make entries for the dollar and the photograph you used in your **Elements** table (see page 7).

Image modes

All our images, by default, use the colour system **RGB**. For printed artwork, this needs to be converted to **CMYK**. You cannot do this in Fireworks, which is a web-based graphics program and uses a system dealing only with screen colours (RGB). Fireworks has five different colour modes from which you can choose and pick colours. Some of these colour modes are outdated simply because modern screens can display millions of colours. Here is a brief explanation of the five main colour modes that you may come across in the world of graphics and printing.

RGB mode

Figure 16.13: A picture in RGB mode

This is a default mode for nearly all images created on the computer. **RGB** uses three colours (also called channels) to reproduce more than 16 million colours, many more than the human eye can distinguish.

The three colours – **Red**, **Green** and **Blue** – are mixed in values of 0–255. If all three colours are set to zero the result is black, and if they are set to 255 the result is white.

Indexed Colour mode

Figure 16.14: A picture in Indexed Colour mode

This mode uses up to 256 colours.

If you convert an **RGB** file to an **Indexed** file, the file size will decrease but the image quality will also be reduced because it has fewer colours. It has to approximate some of the **RGB** colours. **GIF** files use indexed colours.

Greyscale mode

In Greyscale mode this image is 94k.

Figure 16.15: A picture in Greyscale mode

Greyscale uses up to 256 shades of grey. You can scan an image in **Greyscale** mode.

Bitmap mode

In Bitmap mode this image is 12k.

Figure 16.16: A picture in Bitmap mode

Bitmap mode assigns one of two colours (black or white) to each pixel in an image. This results in very small file sizes but unless your image is black and white (text, for example), it will be severely degraded if you save it as a **Bitmap**.

CMYK mode

In CMYK mode this image is 377k.

Figure 16.17: A picture in CMYK mode

CMYK (**Cyan**, **Magenta**, **Yellow** and **black**) is the printing world standard – Fireworks will not allow you to convert to **CMYK**! These are the colours of printer's inks and digitally they are mixed from 0 to 100. If you are converting **RGB** files to **CMYK** in another piece of software, be aware that bright blues and greens will suffer 'drop off', because the inks cannot print colours as bright as your monitor can display!

Changing Image Modes

Whenever you convert a file to a lower quality colour mode (for example from **RGB** to **Indexed Colour**), you should always save a backup in the original mode. You should also aim to do as much editing as possible in the higher quality colour mode before converting.

Hotspots, Slices and Rollovers

In this chapter you will be introduced to some of Fireworks' web-based tools. You can create hotspots, buttons and links in applications such as Dreamweaver, but sometimes it is more convenient to create them in Fireworks and, if necessary, edit them later in website design software.

Hotspots

A hotspot is an area marked out by you so that when the mouse pointer is moved over that area an action is performed. Embedded information will take you to another web page or picture. The embedded information that performs the action is called a **hyperlink**.

We will draw a hotspot and link it to a website, which we can preview in a browser.

◉ Create a new canvas with a **Width** of **800 Pixels**, a **Height** of **600 Pixels**, a **Resolution** of **72 Pixels/Inch** and set the **Canvas color** to **White**.

◉ Draw a vector **Rectangle** and **Star** on the canvas, as shown in Figure 17.1.

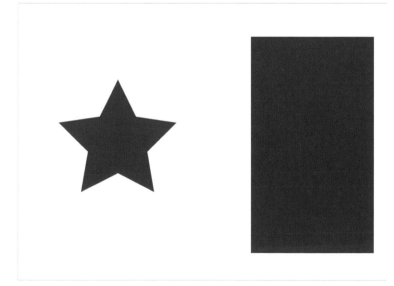

Figure 17.1: Rectangle and star

- In the **Web** section of the **Tools** panel, choose the **Rectangle Hotspot** tool.

- Drag a hotspot over the rectangle shape. You will notice that the hotspot has automatically appeared in the **Web Layer** in the **Layers** panel.

You can draw elliptical and custom-shaped hotspots with the **Polygon Hotspot** tool.

Figure 17.2: Hotspot tools

- Pick the **Polygon Hotspot** tool. Click around the star shape.

- Use the **Subselection** tool if you need to tweak the shape.

Look in the **Layers** panel. You can show and hide each hotspot by using the **Show/Hide** icon next to the object. You can also hide hotspots with the icon in the **Web** section of the **Tools** panel.

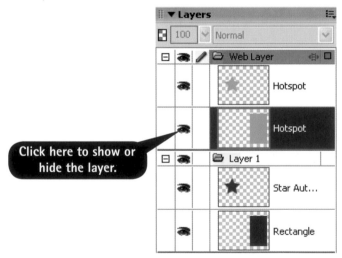

Figure 17.3: Showing and hiding layers

- With the **Pointer** tool, click on the **Rectangle Hotspot** and look in the **Properties inspector**.

Creating a hyperlink

First look at the field called **Link**. We will add a **URL** (uniform resource locator), which will tell the browser to perform an action.

○ Type **http://www.google.co.uk**. (The **http** stands for **HyperText Transfer Protocol**.) This is the link that will send you to a new web page.

Alt text

The next field is **Alt** field, which specifies the alternative text that will appear while an image is loading or if it cannot be loaded. This text is often displayed by your pointer when you hover over an image on a web page.

○ Write **Search engine** in the field.

Target

The **Target** field is the window or frame in which you want the link to open. The choices are:

None and **_self**   opens the destination page in the same location the button is in

_blank   opens the destination page in a new browser window

parent   opens the destination page in the parent frameset of the link

_top   replaces all the frames in the current browser window and opens the destination page in that window.

○ Set **Target** to **_blank** so it opens a new browser window.

Figure 17.4: Properties inspector for the rectangle hotspot

○ Click the **Star Hotspot** and enter a web address of your own. I entered mine and put a very uncool tag.

Figure 17.5: Properties inspector for the star hotspot

> **Tip:** There is also a **Color** box where you can change the colour of the hotspot. This is quite useful if the hotspot is blending into an image.

○ You can view your handiwork by going to **File, Preview in Browser, Preview in iexplore. exe (F12** for a shortcut).

The hotspots are now invisible. When you hover your pointer over one of the hotspots its Alt text appears as a tooltip. Clicking a hotspot opens the target website in a new window.

◐   Close all of the Microsoft Internet Explorer windows, save your image as **RectangleAndStar.png** in your **Exercises** folder and close it.

Creating a button

Making buttons in Fireworks is easy and you can make them change appearance when they are rolled over or pressed. You can add behaviours to display pictures and more. This will give your websites a lot more interactivity and make them much more fun to use.

Often, if you are looking around a website, you will notice that the buttons and other images or text react as the mouse pointer drifts over them – this is a **rollover** and generally indicates that something will happen if you click the button, image or text.

Although Fireworks has lots of ready-made buttons, it is easier to understand how they work by making one.

◐   Create a new canvas with a **Width** of **800 Pixels**, a **Height** of **600 Pixels**, a **Resolution** of **72 Pixels/Inch** and the **Canvas color** set to **White**.

◐   Go to **Edit**, **Insert**, **New Button**.

The **Button Editor** opens, ready to create a new button. The first four tabs across the top of the editor window enable you to select which state you will create the button in. You will create your button in the **Up** state.

Figure 17.6: Button Editor

○ Draw a perfect vector **circle** in the middle of the **Button Editor**, colour it blue and add a **Bevel** from the **live filters**.

○ Use the **Text** tool to write **Yes!** on the button.

○ Use the **Properties inspector** to centre the text in its box.

Figure 17.7

The button should look like Figure 17.8.

Figure 17.8: Button with bevel and text

If you want the button to look different when it is clicked or when the mouse pointer passes over it, you have to create a button for each state.

○ At the top of the canvas, click the **Over** tab. This next button will be displayed when the mouse pointer goes over it. Press the **Copy Up Graphic** button at the bottom right of the canvas to start with a copy of the button in its **Up** state.

○ Select the text and add a **live filter** of type **Shadow and Glow**, **Glow** to make a white glow for the text.

○ Now press the **Down** tab, to specify what you will see when the button is pressed. Click the **Copy Over Graphic** button. Select the vector button and use the **Edit and arrange live filters** icon to change the bevel so that it looks as though the button has been pressed.

○ Go to the **Over While Down** and **Copy Over Graphic**. Change the glow to green.

◉ This is what each button should look like. Click the **Up**, **Over**, **Down** and **Over While Down** tabs to compare your buttons with Figure 17.9.

Figure 17.9: All the different states of the new button

◉ When you are happy with your design, click the **Done** button.

◉ Press **F12** to have a look at your button in Microsoft Internet Explorer. Press **F5** to reset the button.

> **Tip**: You may get the message **To help protect your security, Internet Explorer has restricted this file from showing active content that could access your computer. Click here for options…** You can click and select **Allow blocked content**. Click **Yes** in the pop-up window.

◉ Close the browser window.

Editing a button

◉ To edit your button, double-click it with the **Pointer** tool to return to the **Button Editor**. You can make any changes to your button now.

◉ Click the **Active Area** tab. Fireworks automatically sets a rectangular active area to cover your button. The active area is represented by a **slice** that appears on your screen as a semi-opaque rectangle.

◉ Select the button (or the active area surrounding it) and look in the **Properties inspector**. You will see you can control it just like a hotspot. You don't need to add a hyperlink now.

◉ Press **Done**.

◉ Save the file as **RolloverButton.png** in your **Exercises** folder.

Sharing symbols

When you build a website, you will almost certainly need a navigation bar. This will contain several buttons of a similar appearance, which link the user to different pages in the website. You can very quickly create more buttons that look similar to the one you have just created.

◉ Open **RolloverButton** if it is not still open.

◉ Click the **Library** tab in your **Assets** panel in the **Panel** dock. (If the **Assets** panel is not visible, go to **Window**, **Library** in the **Menu** bar.) In there you will see the **Button** symbol.

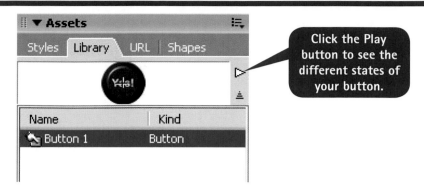

Figure 17.10: Library

◉ Click and drag the button into the canvas.

This creates a duplicate button. You can change the text on the button and the link in the **Properties inspector**. Any other changes (such as the bevel or filter) that you make to either button in the **Button Editor** will be applied to both these buttons. Try this as follows.

◉ In the **Properties inspector**, change the **Text** to **No!** then press **Enter**.

Figure 17.11: Editing the button

The text on the button has changed.

◉ Double-click the button with the **Pointer** tool to enter the **Button Editor**. (The original button will appear, whichever button you double-click.) Change the **Down State** glow to another colour. Press **Done**.

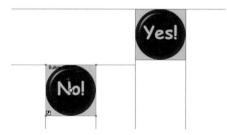

Figure 17.12: Further editing

◉ Press **F12** to view your buttons in the browser to see what happens.

Both of the buttons have changed, as they are linked!

This is very useful when you have a set of similar buttons in a navigation bar – if you want to change, say, the colour or size of the buttons, you only need to do this once for each button state.

Creating an unlinked copy of the button

Sometimes you may want a similar button which has, for example, a different colour from those in the navigation bar. You can create a copy of the button and edit it independently of the others, as follows.

○ In the **Library** drag the button (the name, not the thumbnail) down onto the **New Symbol** icon.

○ The **Symbol Properties** dialogue box appears. Set the **Name** to **ColouredButton**, make sure the **Type** is set to **Button** and press **OK**.

Figure 17.13: Symbol Properties

○ Drag the new button onto the canvas.

○ Double-click the button with the **Pointer** tool to enter the **Button Editor**. Change the colour of the button to red in all four button states and press **F12** to view your buttons in a browser again.

Figure 17.14: Two linked buttons and one unlinked button

○ Save the file as **RolloverButtonV2** in your **Exercises** folder.

○ Close the file.

Creating a disjointed rollover

○ Create a new canvas with a **Width** of **800 Pixels**, a **Height** of **600 Pixels**, a **Resolution** of **72 Pixels/Inch** and the **Canvas color** set to **White**.

This time we will create a disjointed rollover, which is a simple way of making images appear when you want them to.

This involves four steps.

1.   Create two frames with different images to display **before** and **after** the rollover is put into action.

2.   Mark out with a **slice** object where the image is to be viewed.

3.   Add a **hotspot** to trigger the rollover.

4.   Assign a **swap image** behaviour to the trigger object.

Let's do it!

Step 1 – Creating two frames with different images

◉   Click **File**, **Import** (or press **Crtl-R**) to import an image and find **CatamaranSailing.jpg** from your **DownloadedImages** folder.

◉   Draw out the image into the canvas, leaving plenty of room around it.

Figure 17.15: Imported catamaran picture

◉   With the **Text** tool, write **Before** just under the picture.

◉   Go to **Window**, **Frames** to display the **Frames** panel in the **Panel** dock.

◉   Drag **Frame 1** down onto the **New/Duplicate Frame** icon.

◉   Apply a **live filter** of type **Blur**, **Zoom Blur** to the image (not the text) in **Frame 2**. Change the text to **After**.

Step 2 – Marking out a Slice object

⊙ With the **Slice** tool from the **Web** section of the **Tools** panel, draw a slice over the image and the text. Don't worry too much about accuracy – this is just a practice exercise.

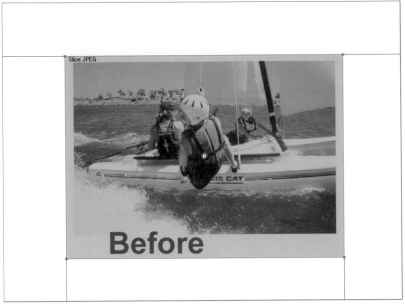

Figure 17.16: Slice

⊙ Select **Window, URL** to display the **URL** panel and set the **Current URL** to **No URL (noHREF)**.

Figure 17.17: URL

⊙ Make sure **Frame 1** is selected in the **Frames** panel.

⊙ Draw a vector **Arrow** (one of the shapes sharing a button with the vector **Rectangle**) in the white area of the canvas. Use the **Scale** tool to rotate the arrow so that it points down to the top left corner of the image (as shown in Figure 17.18, but without the blue hotspot rectangle).

Step 3 – Adding a hotspot to trigger the rollover

⊙ You can easily add a hotspot. With the vector arrow selected, go to **Edit, Insert, Hotspot**.

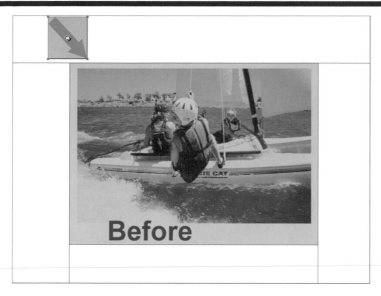

Figure 17.18: The rollover so far

Step 4 – Assigning a Swap Image behaviour to the trigger object

◖ In the centre of the hotspot is a crosshair icon called the **Behavior controller**. Click on it, then drag away from the hotspot and a line will appear.

This is the Behavior controller.
Click on it and drag out from it, and a line will appear.

Figure 17.19: The Behavior controller

◖ Drag the line onto the **Target slice area** (the catamaran image) and release the mouse.

◖ A **Swap Image** dialogue box will appear – click **OK**.

Figure 17.20: Swap Image box

The curved line shows there is a **Swap Image** behaviour between the hotspot and the slice.

◖ Press **F12** to **Preview in Browser** and have a look at what you have done. As your mouse pointer rolls over the arrow, it shows the image on **Frame 2** – simple!

Figure 17.21: The rollover effect

○ Close the browser window.

Behaviors panel

Let's have a quick look at the **Behaviors** panel and what it has to offer.

○ Click on the arrow hotspot.

○ If the **Behaviors** panel is not visible, click **Window**, **Behaviors** to display it.

○ Click on **Events** and change it from the default **onMouseOver** to **onClick**. Press **F12** to see how the change has affected your trigger arrow.

Figure 17.22: Behaviors panel

○ So that you really understand what is going on, draw another vector **Arrow** on **Layer 1** (see Figure 17.24). With the new arrow selected, click **Edit**, **Insert**, **Hotspot**.

○ Click on the **Hotspot** and click and drag the **Behavior controller** onto the **Slice** to create a **Swap Image** behaviour between them.

○ Set the **Swap Image** window to **Frame 1** and click **OK**.

- Click on the first arrow, click the **Options** button in the top right of the **Behaviors** panel and click **Edit**.

- Uncheck **Restore image onMouseOut**. This will mean that the image will remain on **Frame 2** after the mouse pointer leaves the hotspot. Click **OK**.

- Click on the new arrow hotspot and, in the **Behaviors** panel, make sure **Events** is set to **onClick**.

- Click the **Options** button in the top right of the **Behaviors** panel and click **Edit**.

- Set the **Frame no.** to **Frame 1**. Uncheck **Restore image onMouseOut**. This will cause the image to remain on **Frame 2** once clicked. Click **OK**.

 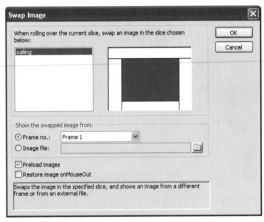

Figure 17.23: Swap Image panels for (a) the first arrow and (b) the second arrow

- Press **F12** and you will find that you now need to click each arrow to switch between **Before** and **After**.

Figure 17.24: Changing between Before and After

- Save your experiment as **DisjointedRollover.png** in your **Exercises** file and close it.

Building a Web Page

In this chapter we are going to build the web page for Base Camp. We will try to make an interactive page that is interesting and a good advertisement for Base Camp.

We have already created a brochure cover as an exercise and this cover will make a very good basis for a striking web page – there's no point letting a perfectly good piece of artwork go to waste!

○ Open **BrochureFrontAndBackCover.png**.

○ Go to **Modify, Canvas, Image size**. The first step is to re-size the image to **800 pixels** wide. The height will automatically change to **567**. Press **OK**.

Figure 18.1: Resizing the image

Tip: A good average web page size is 800 x 600 pixels.

○ Save this as **BaseCampWebPage.png** in your **WebPage** folder.

Creating the text banner

You will make the text **Human tested for fun and adventure** into a banner stretching across the top of the web page.

- ◗ Select the text and move it to the top of the page.

- ◗ Select **Stretch alignment** in the **Properties inspector** and stretch the banner between the guides by dragging its blue selection handles. Change the font size so the height is appropriate for the new width.

- ◗ Add a rounded rectangle and place it under the text.

- ◗ Bring your **BaseCampBunny** in and place it in your banner. You could add another rounded rectangle to change the shape of your banner (see Figure 18.2).

Figure 18.2: Banner on the page

Tip: You will need to drag the **BaseCampBunny** to the **Text** layer.

- ◗ You can save your banner so that you can reuse it on another page. Hold down the **Ctrl** key while you click on each of the four components that make up the banner in the **Layers** panel: the text, the bunny and the two rounded rectangles. Then press **Ctrl-C** to copy.

- ◗ Now go to **File**, **New** and Fireworks will automatically open a canvas with the banner size, so you can press **OK**.

- ◗ Press **Ctrl-V** to paste and then save the banner as **BaseCampBanner.png** in your **WebPage** folder.

Figure 18.3: Finished banner on its own

- ◗ Close the banner and return to **BaseCampWebPage.png**.

Creating different frames

Be careful when doing this next bit – **Layers** and **Frames** are different!

We are going to create four rollovers so that when the mouse pointer rolls over one of the thumbnail images on the left, a larger image appears in place of the logo on the right-hand side.

The first step is to put each of these images into a different frame. The image with the logo is currently in **Frame 1**.

- ◉ In the **Frames and History** panel, drag **Frame 1** on to the **New/Duplicate Frame** icon to create **Frame 2**.

- ◉ Go to the **Layers** panel and switch off the **Base Camp Logo**.

- ◉ Go to **File**, **Open** to open the first image: **CatamaranSailing.png**.

Figure 18.4: Opening images

- ◉ Make sure the image is flattened by going to **Modify**, **Flatten Layers**. If there is more than one object in the layer, select all the objects and go to **Modify**, **Flatten Selection**.

- ◉ Copy the image.

- ◉ Return to **BaseCampWebPage.png**.

- ◉ With the layer containing your background images selected, click **Edit**, **Paste**. If the message shown in Figure 18.5 appears, click **Don't Resample**.

Figure 18.5

➤ Use the **Scale** tool to position and size the image in the right-hand window in place of the logo.

Figure 18.6: Scale tool

➤ To see what you have created, click on **Frame 1** in the **Frames** panel. The logo reappears.

➤ Click on **Frame 2** and the catamaran appears.

➤ Drag **Frame 2** onto the **New/Duplicate Frame** icon to create **Frame 3**.

➤ Make sure **Frame 3** is selected.

➤ Delete the catamaran picture.

➤ Repeat the steps to put **HighLeapSky.png** from your **Exercises** folder into the right-hand window.

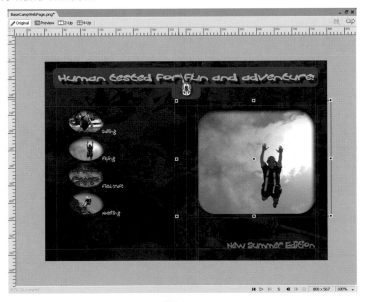

Figure 18.7: Leap!

○ Do the same for the third image, **WoodSign.png**.

○ You can copy and paste **Abseiling.jpg** in the same way, or read the tip below for a faster method.

> **Tip**: If your image is an original photograph, it will not have different layers. You can save time by importing the **jpg** image. With your graphics layer selected, click **File**, **Import** to import **Abseiling.jpg**.

Creating the slices

───○ Use the **Slice** tool to draw a slice over the right-hand window (it doesn't matter which frame and layer are selected).

Figure 18.8: Drawing a slice over the image

Creating hotspots

Next you will create the hotspots for each thumbnail.

○ In the thumbnail layer, click on the **Sailing** thumbnail.

○ Go to **Edit**, **Insert**, **Hotspot**.

○ Create hotspots for the other three thumbnails.

───○ Use the **Subselection** tool to move or resize any of the hotspot boxes that are overlapping.

Figure 18.9: Making sure that the hotspots don't overlap

The hotspots have been automatically placed on the web layer.

◐   Re-name the hotspots **Sailing**, **Flying**, **FieldCraft** and **Abseiling**.

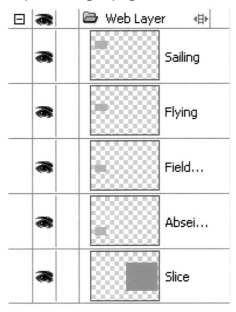

Figure 18.10: Naming the hotspots

Assigning a swap image behaviour

◐   **Drag** the cross-hair from the centre of the first hotspot to the right-hand window (the target slice area). A **Swap Image** dialogue box will appear.

◉ Select **Frame 2** (the catamaran picture) and click **OK**.

Figure 18.11: Swap Image

◉ Repeat this process for each thumbnail, selecting frames 3, 4 and 5.

Figure 18.12: Assigning swap image behaviour

◉ Press **F12** to test your rollovers.

◉ When you've taken in the beauty and genius of your creation, close the browser window.

◉ Save as **BaseCampWebPage.png** in your **WebPage** folder.

Spell checker!

It is a good idea to check your spelling. You can select a word with the **Text** tool and go to **Text**, **Check Spelling**.

If you have not set up a language, then you will get a **Spelling Setup** window like the one shown in Figure 18.13.

Figure 18.13: Spelling Setup

○ Press **OK**.

○ When you run the **Check Spelling** function, you will get a **Check Spelling** window like Figure 18.14 if Fireworks finds a mistake. Select the correct spelling and choose **Change**.

Figure 18.14: Check Spelling

The spell checker will even check your layer names, so it is very useful. It will tell you when it is complete and you can then click **OK** to finish.

○ Save your work as **BaseCampWebPage.png** in your **WebPage** folder when you are happy with the page.

Now put all of your new skills to good use and enjoy using Fireworks. You could even learn to use these skills to make fantastic Flash or Dreamweaver games, graphics and websites!

Index